US MILITARY ENCYCLOPEDIAS

THE ARMED FORCES ENCYCLOPEDIA

BY TAMMY GAGNE

Encyclopedias

An Imprint of Abdo Reference

abdobooks.com

TABLE OF CONTENTS

THE HISTORY OF THE US MILITARY

The United States has had a military since before the country was formally established. The Continental Army formed when American colonists came together to fight Great Britain for independence in the American Revolution (1775–1783). Their success led to the creation of a new country. The US military has grown since the early days of independence and remains a source of pride for many people in the United States. The men and women of today's military continue to protect and defend the United States at home and overseas.

A GROWING MILITARY

In the early days of the United States, most military members were white men. However, historians estimate that about 5,000 Black

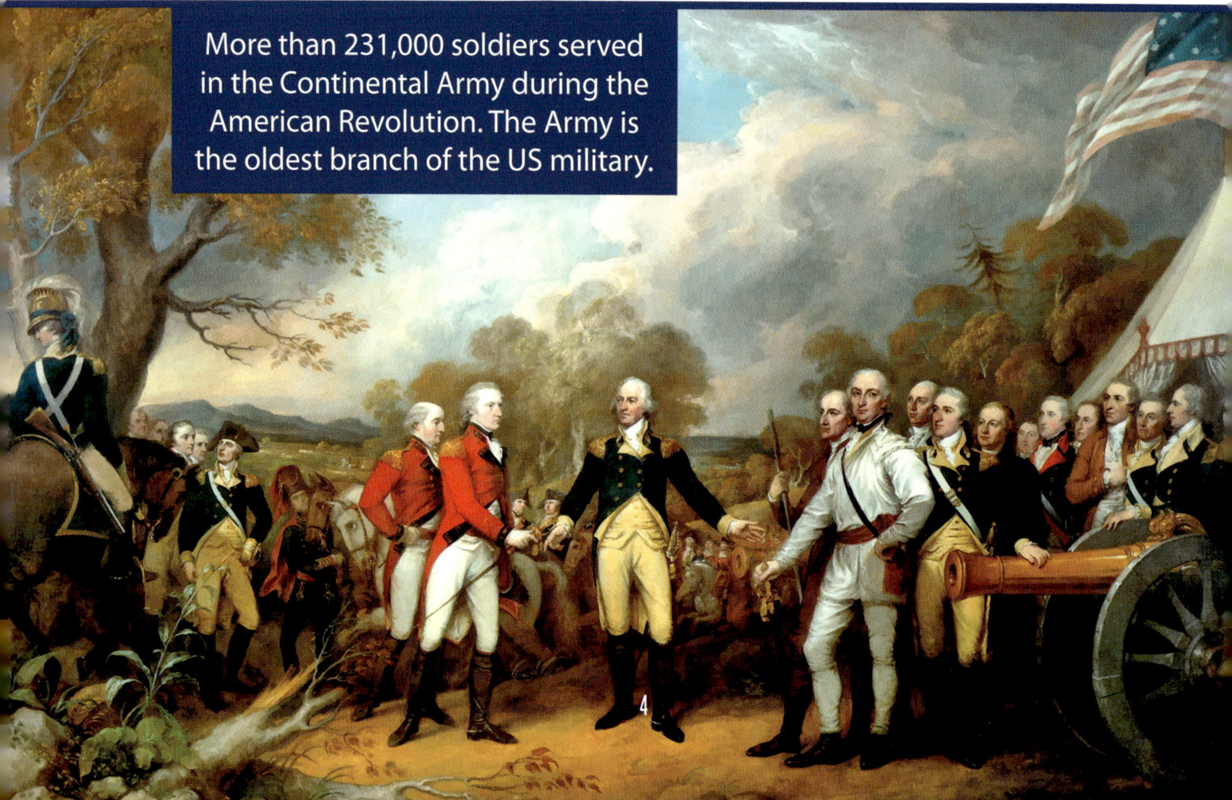

More than 231,000 soldiers served in the Continental Army during the American Revolution. The Army is the oldest branch of the US military.

men served in the Continental Army during the Revolutionary War. A 1792 federal law prohibited Black men from enlisting in the US armed forces. White men worried that giving enslaved Black people access to guns and other weapons would lead to a rebellion. They also thought Black men might want freedom in exchange for their service. In 1862, in the midst of the American Civil War (1861–1865), President Abraham Lincoln issued the Emancipation Proclamation. This freed some enslaved people in the United States. It also gave Black men the right to serve in the US military.

Women were also barred from joining the armed forces for many years. But in 1948, President Harry S. Truman signed the Women's Armed Services Integration Act. This law allowed women to serve as full-time service members of all military branches.

As the country grew, more people were allowed to serve in the military. The modern military is much more diverse than in the past. Approximately 43 percent of US military members identified as minorities in 2017. In 2023, women made up 16 percent of all service members.

The US military began with just one branch: the Army. The military now includes six branches. They are the US Air Force, the US Army, the US Coast Guard, the US Marine Corps, the US Navy, and the US Space Force. Each of these military branches has its own responsibilities.

US AIR FORCE

Until the early 1900s, wars were fought mainly on land and at sea. The winning side usually had the most powerful army or navy. The settings for war expanded in 1914. This was when World War I (1914–1918) began in Europe.

Aircraft technology was still relatively new. But planes offered advantages in warfare. Pilots could fly through the sky over their enemies. They could attack from the air and see

Air Force pilots require a lot of training in air navigation and aircraft operations.

The P-51 Mustang, *top*, and Vought F4U, *bottom*, are two types of planes that the US military used during World War II.

enemy movements from far away. After they landed, pilots could tell their ground commanders what was happening so they could prepare. Toward the end of World War I, radios were added to planes. This made communication between the air and ground quicker and easier.

Aircraft played an even greater role in World War II (1939–1945). Many nations used planes to watch their enemies and gather information. Militaries, including the US military, also used more planes for combat. Planes were armed with machine guns and bombs. The weapons allowed wars to be fought from the sky. Planes were also used to carry important supplies, such as food and medical supplies, to soldiers.

By the end of the war, the United States had built nearly 300,000 aircraft for its military. But there wasn't a US military branch dedicated solely to airpower at this time. Pilots and planes were under the command of the US Army.

The Department of the Air Force was created when Congress passed the National Security Act of 1947. William Stuart Symington was sworn in as the secretary of the Air Force on September 18, becoming the head of the department. Symington worked to help manage funding for the new department. Airplane technology was developing quickly, with innovations such as jet engines and radar becoming standard. The Air Force would need to build new planes and other advanced equipment to defend the nation in the event of another war. The Air Force would also need to train more pilots.

Members of the Air Force help transport medical supplies and equipment to Turkey following a major earthquake in 2023.

A member of the Air Force wraps up a fuel hose. The Air Force includes many careers in maintenance and repairs.

Air Force members are led by the branch's chief of staff. This person's primary responsibilities include the organization and training of Air Force members. General Carl A. Spaatz became the first person to serve in this position on September 26, 1947. His background included serving as a combat pilot during World War I.

The modern Air Force has several responsibilities that have grown since the founding of the military branch. It is responsible for establishing a strong presence in the air by maintaining aircraft and developing aviation technology. The Air Force also has duties in protecting US interests in space. As in the past, the Air Force uses aircraft to gather information from its enemies. The military branch values its ability to respond quickly to

In 2023, the US Air Force chief of staff was General Charles Q. Brown Jr. He was promoted to the position in 2020.

The Air Force has jobs related to science and technology. Airmen can work to develop technology for rocket engines.

disasters around the world. Additionally, the Air Force is a major part of US military power and strategy.

Like other branches of the armed forces, the Air Force has both military jobs and jobs for civilians. Civilians may work in administrative roles that help keep the Air Force organized and running effectively. They may work in careers related to science and health care. Engineers help develop and maintain aircraft. The Air Force is also involved with cyberspace security and weather forecasting.

An Air Force plane dropped fire retardant to slow the spread of a California wildfire in 2017.

Combat Controllers run back to shore during a training exercise. They are expected to be able to run at least 1.5 miles (2.4 km).

AIR FORCE SPECIAL FORCES

The US military has several special forces groups. Special forces members receive additional training so they can perform difficult missions. The Air Force has four special operations forces: Combat Control, Pararescue, Special Reconnaissance, and the Tactical Air Control Party.

Combat Controllers work with special forces teams in other branches of the military, including Army Rangers and Navy SEALs. Combat Controllers are often sent to some of the most dangerous war zones in the world. They direct the movement of combat aircraft. Their work helps coordinate the timing of attacks. Arriving too early or too late for these

Combat Controllers may be expected to parachute while on duty.

Pararescue specialists might be called upon to help astronauts who have returned to Earth from missions in space.

missions can mean the difference between success and failure. Combat Controllers also help prevent aircraft collisions.

These special forces members are trained to perform a variety of challenging tasks themselves. They may need to scuba dive, parachute, or even snowmobile to reach certain destinations. Like other special forces careers, work as a Combat Controller is both mentally and physically demanding.

Pararescue specialists are trained to treat a wide range of injuries. They are responsible for providing aid to military members and civilians who are injured or trapped in remote or hostile areas. Like Combat Controllers, these special forces members are trained to scuba dive and parachute to reach people who need them. They may even need to climb mountains or travel through arctic conditions.

Information is one of the most valuable tools of the military. Similar to the World War I pilots who watched their enemies from the sky, today's Air Force gathers information to gain advantages in war. Members of Air Force Special Reconnaissance are responsible for this task. They gather information such as an enemy force's position and movements.

Pararescue specialists may need to hoist wounded soldiers or civilians into an aircraft.

Drones allow the Air Force to survey terrain and collect information in areas where it may be dangerous to send people.

This information can help the US military strategize plans for attack or prepare its defenses. Special Reconnaissance members share this information with other military branches.

Air Force Special Reconnaissance members often use drones to collect information. But members may need to enter enemy territory themselves. These Air Force members receive special training that prepares them to parachute into dangerous territory. Special Reconnaissance members help the Air Force gather information from the ground. They may use techniques such as cyber warfare or electronic warfare to accomplish their missions.

Reconnaissance helps members of a Tactical Air Control Party plan air strikes. Successful air strikes can turn the tide of a war. Members of a Tactical Air Control Party go through extensive training. They must learn to identify targets for air strikes and plan when strikes would be most effective. A Tactical Air Control Party coordinates attacks with Army and Marine units. After an air strike, these military forces can move in to perform their roles in an operation.

Members of a Tactical Air Control Party direct aircraft from the ground to accomplish successful offensive strikes.

Tactical Air Control members use laser targeting devices, night vision, and thermal imaging equipment to pinpoint their targets. Much of the work performed by Tactical Air Control members is done on the ground so they can better coordinate attacks between land and air forces. They are responsible for relaying information to thousands of individuals. They must have strong communication skills and an understanding of strategy and military technology.

FAMOUS AIR FORCE MEMBERS

The Air Force has had many remarkable members. One of them was Billy Mitchell. Often called the Father of the Air Force, Mitchell began his military career in the Army in 1898. He became commander of Army Aviation in 1916. In World War I, he commanded the US aerial combat units in France as a brigadier general. Mitchell often spoke out about the need for a separate US Air Force. He died in 1936, but the military acknowledged his contributions to US airpower. A bomber called the B-25 Mitchell was named in his honor.

Charles "Chuck" Elwood Yeager is another famous Air Force member. He made history in October 1947 as the first pilot to fly faster than the speed of sound. People refer to this accomplishment

The US military flew B-25 Mitchell aircraft during World War II. Many of these planes are on display in museums, and some are still capable of flight.

as breaking the sound barrier. Yeager reached a speed of 700 miles per hour (1,127 kmh) during the flight.

PLANES IN WORLD WAR II

The Air Force has played a significant role in numerous wars and conflicts around the world. Though the Air Force was not yet established during World War II, aircraft still contributed

In 2012, Chuck Yeager, *center*, spoke to US airmen after they completed a flight celebrating the 65th anniversary of Yeager breaking the sound barrier.

An Air Force technician inspects the radar system of an aircraft. Radar technology played an important role in World War II.

significantly to the war. The United States joined the Allies in 1941. The Allies included nations such as the United Kingdom and the Soviet Union. They fought against the Axis powers, which included Japan, Germany, and Italy.

Much of World War II was fought from the air. More than 30 nations took part in the conflict. US airpower played a major role in bringing the war to an end. US military aircraft dropped atomic bombs on the Japanese cities of Hiroshima and Nagasaki in August 1945. These attacks killed more than 200,000 Japanese people and prompted Japan to surrender.

This is a model of the atomic bomb, called Fat Man, that was dropped on Nagasaki, Japan, in World War II.

Japan's leaders signed documents to officially end World War II on September 2, 1945.

TUSKEGEE AIRMEN

Between 1941 and 1946, approximately 1,000 airmen trained at the Tuskegee Institute in Alabama. The Tuskegee Institute, which is now Tuskegee University, was a historically Black college. It was founded to provide career opportunities and education to Black people.

Before the pilot training program was established at the Tuskegee Institute, no Black person had ever served as a pilot for the US military. The graduates of this program who served in World War II were known as the Tuskegee Airmen. Many of them were awarded for their service. The Tuskegee Airmen served separately from white members of the Army Air Forces.

Their efforts helped pave the way to ending segregation in the US military.

In 1975, Daniel "Chappie" James Jr. became the first Black four-star general in the US military. James had received his pilot certification at the Tuskegee Institute. He then instructed

Before 1948, Black people served in separate units from white members of the military.

other pilots there. James didn't serve as a fighter pilot himself until the Korean War (1950–1953), during which he flew 101 combat missions. James also flew 78 missions in the Vietnam War (1954–1975).

Daniel James Jr., *center*, received stars marking him as major general in the Air Force on July 31, 1972.

Aircraft transported wounded soldiers from combat areas during the Korean War.

THE AIR FORCE IN THE KOREAN WAR

Another international conflict began in the early 1950s. Communist leaders in North Korea wanted to take over noncommunist South Korea. In 1950, the Korean People's

Army of North Korea invaded South Korea. It seemed that North Korea would take control. Worried about the spread of communism, the United States entered the Korean War and supported South Korea.

The Air Force played a key role in helping South Korea throughout the conflict. US pilots were more experienced than pilots from North Korea. The US Air Force was able to limit North Korean presence in the air. Without air control, North Korea was unable to take control of South Korea. When the war ended three years later, South Korea remained independent.

The Korean War Veterans Memorial in Washington, DC, honors the people who served in that conflict.

During the Vietnam War, the Air Force dropped bombs as part of Operation Arc Light.

THE AIR FORCE IN THE VIETNAM WAR

Like the Korean War, the Vietnam War was fought primarily over communism. North Vietnam supported communism while South Vietnam opposed it. Early in the war, the US Air Force trained South Vietnamese pilots. But by the late 1960s, the United States had become directly involved in the conflict. It provided South Vietnam with equipment, such as weapons. Americans also fought on the front lines. While the US Army made its way through jungles, the Air Force took to the sky.

The Air Force prevented North Vietnam from taking over in the south. It launched Operation Linebacker I, which lasted

The Air Force targeted bridges and other transportation lines during the Vietnam War to limit North Vietnam's ability to move weapons and other products.

from May to October 1972. During this operation, the Air Force dropped more than 150,000 tons (136,080 metric tons) of bombs on North Vietnam. In addition to stopping enemy combatants, the bombings also made it difficult for North Vietnamese troops to receive supplies.

The Air Force also spread an herbicide called Agent Orange as part of Operation Ranch Hand. Herbicides contain chemicals that harm plants. The US military used Agent Orange for two main reasons. First, Agent Orange caused the leaves to fall from trees, making it easier to spot the enemy in Vietnam's dense jungles. Second, the US military wanted to destroy the enemy's crops to further weaken their troops.

A chemical in Agent Orange caused millions of people who were exposed to the herbicide to develop health

The Vietnam Veterans Memorial near the Washington Monument in Washington, DC, lists the names of more than 58,000 people who died in service during the war.

problems, such as cancer. It also caused birth defects in children who were born after the war. Production of the herbicide stopped in the 1970s for these reasons. But the chemical is still present in the environment and continues to cause health problems in Vietnam and for US veterans.

Airmen sometimes train in jungle conditions so they are prepared to work in this terrain.

People who score well in mechanical operations on the ASVAB may go on to work as maintenance technicians. They make sure aircraft are safe to fly.

JOINING THE AIR FORCE

People interested in joining the Air Force should begin by taking the Armed Services Vocational Aptitude Battery (ASVAB). This series of tests measures a person's strengths and potential for success in the military. It assesses skills in science, language, mechanics, and other fields. The results can show which branch of the military may be a good fit for a person. The ASVAB can provide insight on suitable military or civilian careers within the armed forces. The test is often given at high schools, colleges and universities, and Job Corps centers.

One of the most important parts of the ASVAB is the armed forces qualification test (AFQT), which measures math and reading skills. To be accepted into the Air Force, high

After taking the ASVAB, new recruits are tested on their fitness.

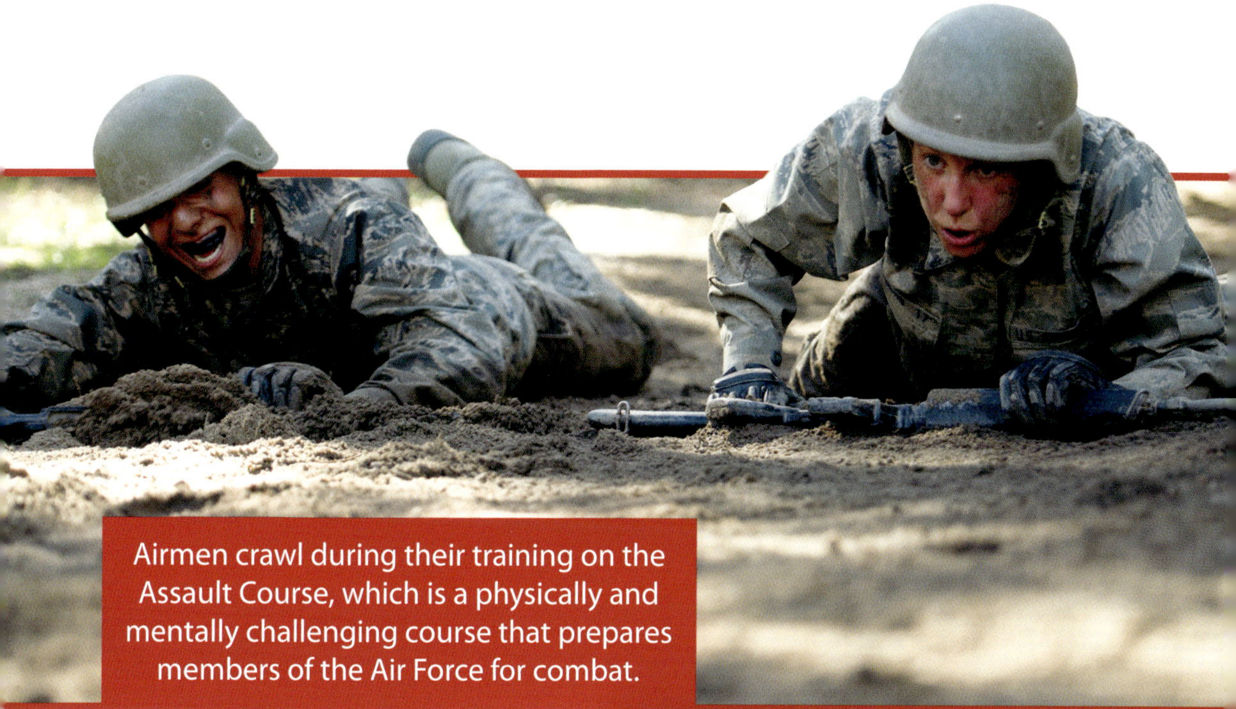

Airmen crawl during their training on the Assault Course, which is a physically and mentally challenging course that prepares members of the Air Force for combat.

school graduates must earn a minimum AFQT score of 31. A person with a general equivalency diploma (GED) must earn a minimum score of 50. The highest possible AFQT score is 99.

Incoming military personnel must fulfill certain physical requirements in order to serve. All branches of the armed forces require physically and mentally intense training for their members, but the specific

Air Force students practice parachuting skills using a swing and landing gear.

requirements and the duration of basic training vary between the branches.

Air Force recruits must go through basic military training (BMT). BMT lasts eight and a half weeks. By the end, male recruits must be able to run 1.5 miles (2.4 km) in 11 minutes and 57 seconds or less. They must complete 42 sit-ups and 27 push-ups in one minute. Female recruits have to run 1.5 miles (2.4 km) in 14 minutes and 26 seconds or less. They have to do 38 sit-ups and 18 push-ups in one minute.

Each year approximately 1,000 people graduate from the US Air Force Academy. Graduates are eligible to join the Air Force or Space Force as officers.

Air Force pharmacists help fill prescriptions and can assist in health care around the world.

After graduating from BMT, most Air Force members receive the rank of airman basic, or E-1. A person's rank rises through promotions, from E-1 to E-9. The *E* stands for enlisted. Common jobs for enlisted airmen include carrying out military operations and maintaining equipment. Higher levels of enlisted airmen may be responsible for supervising lower ranks.

There are multiple ways to become an officer in the US military. Graduates of military academies, such as the US Air Force Academy, automatically become officers. Completing a Reserve Officers' Training Corps (ROTC) program at a college or university is another way. College graduates who did not do ROTC must go to Officer Training School to be an officer in the Air Force. Individuals may be selected to go to this training school after advancing through the enlisted ranks.

Highly trained professionals in medicine, engineering, or other fields may also enter the Air Force as officers.

Some positions in the Air Force are available only to officers. For example, being an officer is a requirement for becoming an Air Force pilot. Other officers serve as engineers, attorneys, personnel managers, or dentists. Officers may serve in positions of authority and command Air Force units. Officers hold positions above the enlisted airmen. Officer ranks start at O-1,

A crew chief communicates with a pilot to ensure that the aircraft is ready for takeoff.

which is a second lieutenant. The *O* stands for officer. The rank O-10 is for generals, the highest rank in the Air Force.

The Air Force includes both active-duty and reserve members. Serving in the Air Force is a full-time job for active-duty members. They can be sent to serve anywhere in the United States. Or they may serve on US bases in other countries.

For members of the Air Force Reserve, service is a part-time job. But in the event of war, reserve members can be called into full-time service. Reserve members usually stay close to home.

Some members of the Air Force specialize in public health. They may be asked to perform food safety inspections and make sure food is stored properly.

But they must spend a minimum of one weekend each month and two weeks each year serving in the Air Force.

The Air Force Reserve and the Air National Guard share some responsibilities, such as responding to natural disasters and state-level emergencies. But the Air Force Reserve and the Air National Guard are different. The Air National Guard is a part-time program. It is a partnership between the US military and the states. Although state governors usually control National Guard members, the program is funded by the federal government. The US president can also call on the National Guard when needed.

Members of the Air Force Reserve must complete basic training. This includes learning how to fight during a chemical attack.

US ARMY

The Army is the oldest branch of the US military. It is older than the United States itself. The Second Continental Congress created this military branch before the start of the American Revolution. At this time, the branch was called the Continental Army. About 230,000 people served in the Continental Army during the American Revolution. Most members had little or no training.

George Washington, *left*, served as the commander of the Continental Army.

The battle at Lexington during the Revolutionary War was one of the first battles between the British Army and the Continental Army.

In the 1760s, Great Britain began increasing the amount of taxes colonists in North America had to pay. Many colonists thought it was unfair to be taxed without proper representation in the British government. This issue ultimately led to the war for independence. To win that war, the colonists needed an army that could stand against the British military, which was one of the most powerful militaries in the world.

Members of the Continental Army were united in their passion for gaining their freedom. The motivation for British forces in the colonies was not as strong. The colonists also knew the North American land better than the British. The Continental Army could use this knowledge to better position troops when defending territory. The Continental Army was equipped to use guerrilla warfare, which involved sending a small group of soldiers to sneak up on and attack opposing forces. Because British soldiers were unfamiliar with the land, they could not use these tactics.

Eventually, the Continental Army received support from several other nations. France, Spain, and the Dutch Republic all took part in the fight against the British. The Continental Army defeated the British at the Battle of Yorktown in 1781.

Since the Revolutionary War, the US Army has fought

Guerilla warfare has been used by the US Army since the American Revolution.

Alliances are important to the US military. In 2015, US soldiers trained with Estonian troops so they could more effectively fight alongside each other in the event of war.

in numerous wars in the United States and around the world. Through these conflicts, the Army has expanded its experience, resources, and size. By World War I, the Army included approximately 127,500 soldiers. During World War II, there were more than 11 million people enlisted in the US Army.

In 2021, the Army had more than 482,000 active-duty members. In addition to its active members, the Army also had more than 184,000 reservists. Active-duty members and reservists all contribute to making the US Army one of the most powerful military branches in the world.

The Army is responsible for training soldiers. These soldiers help preserve peace and build alliances with other countries. They also defend the United States in the event of war by serving in combat operations on land. Counterterrorism is one objective of the Army. Soldiers are expected to gather information and work with members of other military branches to ensure the safety of US citizens.

The Army also provides humanitarian aid. The US government might ask the Army to respond to a natural disaster or assist in other crises, such as

Many vehicles used by the Army have tracks, which allow the vehicles to move more easily on difficult terrain.

Army soldiers may be sent around the world to provide food and health care to people in need.

disease outbreaks or severe famines. Members of the Army provide food, water, and health care to people affected by these conditions.

In addition to military positions, the Army also employs civilians. Many career paths are available. People with experience in cybersecurity, finance, and engineering can find jobs that support the Army.

ARMY SPECIAL FORCES

Special operations forces within the Army receive special training. They carry out the branch's most challenging missions.

The Army's special forces groups are the Army Rangers, the Green Berets, Special Operations Aviation Regiment (SOAR) Night Stalkers, Psychological Operations, and Civil Affairs.

The earliest version of the Army Rangers started before the American Revolution. Robert Rogers was a soldier who fought in the French and Indian War (1754–1763). He learned battle techniques from American Indians who fought alongside him in the war. Rogers raised his own special militia force and taught the members these tactics. This force was known as Rogers's Rangers and would eventually become the Army Rangers.

Modern Army Rangers still follow a list of guidelines that Rogers created called the 28 Rules of Ranging. Like Rogers's

Candidates for the Army special forces push a jeep through the sand as part of an exercise to test whether they are fit for service in the special forces.

Army Rangers climbed cliffs in Pointe du Hoc, France, in honor of a famous World War II battle that took place there.

Rangers, Army Rangers travel deep inside enemy territory. The responsibilities and skills of modern Rangers have evolved since Rogers's time. Army Rangers are trained in close combat skills. They are often required to conduct raids in enemy territory to recover equipment or friendly forces.

Army Rangers must clear an obstacle course as part of their training.

Army Rangers undergo training at Ranger School, where their physical and mental endurance are pushed to the limit. They learn combat skills and gain experience operating in all kinds of terrain, including mountains and waterways. This training prepares them to be stationed around the world.

Like Army Rangers, Green Berets are often sent on missions in enemy territory. While Army Rangers are trained to execute direct attacks, Green Berets are experts in guerrilla warfare. They may work with local resistance groups to overthrow

a government. Green Berets focus on counterterrorism and work to prevent and respond to terrorist attacks.

Although SOAR Night Stalkers are part of the Army, a big part of their job involves flying aircraft. These soldiers are trained to operate some of the most advanced helicopters in existence, such as Black Hawk

Green Berets may be required to storm a building to gather information or prevent terrorist activity.

Members of the Army special forces may use special equipment, such as devices that can see heat.

helicopters. These aircraft are used for organized attacks and other missions. SOAR pilots often fly at night, when they are less likely to be spotted by enemies.

A Chinook helicopter flown by members of a SOAR regiment hovers above US Army troops during a training exercise. Soldiers may be required to quickly climb into or out of a moving aircraft.

They use night vision devices to help them see clearly in the dark.

One of the most important jobs of a Night Stalker is to transport other special operations Army members to and from some of the most dangerous places in the world. Night Stalkers also provide humanitarian aid. They respond to natural disasters and can deliver important cargo, such as food, water, and medical supplies, to affected areas.

Fighting wars and keeping peace are done in many ways. Having a strong army that can win in combat is just one part of being a world power. Communication skills are just as important. Members of the Army's Psychological Operations (PSYOP) are trained to persuade both allies and enemies to make decisions that keep US citizens safe. These

SOAR Night Stalkers can use aircraft to carry small boats.

special forces members learn the languages and study the cultures of the countries where they serve. They use these skills to communicate and connect with people in those nations, which helps influence their thoughts and beliefs.

For example, PSYOP soldiers may use social media to gain support for a US cause. They may use electronic warfare to block radio signals from enemies. These soldiers may also put forth misinformation to confuse enemies. Their methods of weakening enemy forces are less direct than the tactics of Army Rangers and Green Berets.

PSYOP members watch as leaflets are released from their aircraft. The leaflets contain information to persuade civilians in the area to support US operations in fighting rebel forces.

Lieutenant Colonel Mark Martin, the leader of an Army Civil Affairs team, shakes hands with an Afghan leader following a meeting.

Members of Civil Affairs also encourage people in other nations to cooperate with the United States. These Army members use direct diplomacy. They partner with other governments and openly discuss issues that could threaten

relations between the United States and these nations. Civil Affairs soldiers aim to understand and help other countries while encouraging them to work with the United States. They provide humanitarian aid in war zones and in times of peace.

The Civil War was the deadliest war in US history. More than 600,000 people died in the war.

THE ARMY IN THE CIVIL WAR

During the Civil War, the United States split into two over the issue of slavery. President Lincoln wanted to stop the spread of slavery. The Southern states were proslavery. Northern states made up the Union, and Southern states formed the

Rifles were among the most popular weapons used by both armies during the Civil War.

Confederacy. The Army was also divided. Soldiers on both sides of the Civil War had once been part of the US Army. The Union Army, with generals such as Ulysses S. Grant, fought to keep the United States together. The Confederate Army fought for the right to secede, or leave, the United States. The Confederacy wanted to form a new nation that could make its own

In addition to serving as a commanding general for the Union Army, Grant was later elected president of the United States.

economic decisions and allow slavery to continue. One of its key generals was Robert E. Lee.

Army forces played a significant role in the Civil War. While the skills of the Union and Confederate armies were well matched, Union soldiers outnumbered the Confederate soldiers by about two to one. Richmond, Virginia, served as the capital of the Confederacy. It held many weapons and other war supplies. Capturing this city was key to Union victory, but Grant was unable to lead a successful raid of the city at first.

Union soldiers stand with a type of cannon called a mortar. This mortar, which was known as the Dictator, was used during the battle at Petersburg.

Robert E. Lee, *seated left*, signed official documents of surrender, ending the Civil War.

After several bloody battles, Grant turned his attention to the nearby city of Petersburg, which was about 24 miles (39 km) south of Richmond. The Confederacy relied on Petersburg's railway to move ammunition and food into Richmond. The Union Army slowly gained ground. It took more than nine months, but Union soldiers eventually captured Petersburg in early 1865. Without this key city, Richmond was weakened. It lost access to important supplies. The victory at Petersburg put the Union Army in a good position to move into Richmond. Lee was forced to flee the capital, and the Confederacy surrendered soon afterward, on April 9, 1865.

The first US tank was developed during World War I. It was the M1917 Light Tank, which was used by the Army until 1931.

THE ARMY IN WORLD WAR I

World War I brought large numbers of US soldiers across the Atlantic Ocean for the first time. The Central Powers, including Germany and Austria-Hungary, were at war with the Allies, which included the United Kingdom and France. The United States entered the war on the side of the Allies in 1917. It had just 127,500 soldiers at this time.

European forces had been fighting since 1914. US troops provided much-needed assistance, but at first the Army was not prepared to fight overseas. It struggled to get troops and equipment to Europe. While the Army worked to establish better organization and improve mobilization of its troops, US soldiers supported French and British troops.

By the end of the war, the US Army had grown significantly. More than four million people served in this military branch during World War I. The organization of the Army also improved. US Army generals were soon entrusted with leadership and commanded large combined forces in Europe. For example, General John Joseph Pershing led more than one million French and US soldiers in key battles in 1918.

Huge numbers of US troops mobilized during World War I.

He was successful in leading these combined armies to reclaim land from Germany.

Henry Johnson was one of many US soldiers who were recognized for their heroic efforts during World War I. Johnson was part of the American Expeditionary Forces 369th Infantry Regiment. At this time, Black soldiers and white soldiers in the US Army served in separate units. Johnson and the other soldiers in the 369th Regiment were Black.

General Pershing sent the 369th Regiment to serve with a French army unit. When Germans attacked that unit on May 15, 1918, Johnson risked his life to defend his fellow soldiers. He and another soldier

General Pershing was promoted to the rank of General of the Armies during World War I.

Henry Johnson was born in North Carolina on July 15, 1892.

Many of the soldiers in the 369th Regiment came from a neighborhood in New York City called Harlem. The soldiers called themselves the "Harlem Rattlers."

were on a night patrol when they heard a group of German soldiers approaching.

Johnson started throwing grenades at the enemy. He and his fellow soldiers were greatly outnumbered. Johnson's ally was wounded in the attack, and Johnson himself was shot. But he did not back down even when he ran out of grenades. He pulled out his knife, stopping the German troops from capturing his fallen comrade. Johnson forced the Germans to retreat. By the time the attack was over, Johnson had suffered 21 injuries. He took down four German soldiers and wounded as many as 20. Meanwhile, Johnson had saved the life of his ally, and no French or US soldiers were killed or captured in the fight.

Following the war, France awarded Johnson the French Croix de Guerre, which means "war cross," for his role in the combat. The Croix de Guerre is France's highest award for bravery. While Johnson was welcomed back to the United States as a hero, he did not receive US military awards until after his death. Johnson died in 1929 and was buried at Arlington National Cemetery in Washington, DC. He was awarded the Purple Heart in 1996. This medal is given to US soldiers who have been wounded or killed in service. Johnson received the Medal of Honor in 2015. This award is the highest medal a military member can earn in the United States.

More than 11,500 US soldiers received the French Croix de Guerre for their service in World War I.

US troops faced snowy winter conditions in Europe during World War II.

THE ARMY IN WORLD WAR II

Army general George Patton served in both world wars. But it was World War II that made Patton famous. In mid-December 1944, it seemed that the Allies were about to defeat Axis leader Adolf Hitler. Hitler was the leader of Germany and commander in chief of the German military. But Hitler made one final attempt to win the war. He sent German soldiers to Belgium to carry out a surprise attack against the Allied forces stationed there.

US soldiers were the first to fight these German troops. In one encounter, 18 men went up against approximately 500 German paratroopers. The US soldiers were captured, but they were able to delay the advancing German forces. Still, the Germany army used its tanks to push through Allied defenders, creating a bulge in the front lines. This is the reason the battle is known as the Battle of the Bulge.

Despite the surprise attack, the US Army regrouped. It defended Allied territory and prevented German forces from gaining more land. Eventually, US Army troops, including those under Patton, were able to reclaim the bulge of land that Germany had won and force the German troops to retreat. The Allied forces claimed victory by mid-January 1945. It was a turning

General Patton was an expert in tank warfare.

General James McConville, *left*, shook the hand of Darrel Bush, *right*, in 2023. Bush is a World War II veteran who served in the Battle of the Bulge.

point in the war. The Battle of the Bulge was the last major attack Hitler would attempt. Many historians consider the victory in the Battle of the Bulge to be one of the greatest accomplishments of the US Army.

A recruit climbs through an obstacle course as part of basic combat training for the Army.

JOINING THE ARMY

People can continue the legacy of the Army by enlisting. The first step to joining the Army is taking the ASVAB. A minimum AFQT score of 31 is required to serve in the Army. Some jobs in the Army require higher scores on the ASVAB than others.

Enlisted ranks in the Army range from E-1 to E-9, similar to the structure of ranks within the Air Force. E-1, the most basic rank in the Army, is called private. The rank of private is given to Army members when they begin basic combat training (BCT).

During the combat portion of BCT, recruits learn hand-to-hand fighting skills.

Some people with a four-year college degree are eligible to join the Army as an E-4, which is the rank of specialist. They still need to complete BCT.

BCT is also called boot camp. During this ten-week program, privates undergo physical training. They learn hand-to-hand combat techniques and also receive training on how to use various weapons, including rifles and machine guns. Recruits prepare for war by practicing first aid, navigation, and other survival skills.

Officers rank above enlisted Army members. People who graduate from the US Military Academy will automatically enter the Army as an officer. College graduates who have completed their school's ROTC program also become officers. Civilians with high levels of experience in fields such as health care, cybersecurity, and law may be elevated to the rank of officer.

Other enlistees will need additional training to become officers. They can attend Officer Candidate School. This 12-week program tests a person's fitness, leadership, and survival skills.

Members of the Army take part in a training exercise to prepare for working with live weapons.

Cybersecurity protects the Army from cyber threats that can affect weapons systems, communication, and more.

The lowest rank for officers is O-1, which is second lieutenant. The highest rank is O-10, which is general. It takes about 30 years of service for most Army generals to achieve their rank.

In order to join the special forces, additional training is required. After completing BCT, people attend advanced individual training. They also must attend Airborne School, where they learn parachuting techniques. Once these requirements are fulfilled, soldiers are eligible to attend the Special Forces Qualification Course (SFQC). It takes at least 53 weeks to complete this course. It is both physically and mentally demanding. People further develop their weaponry skills and military strategy. People may specialize in areas such as engineering, communications, and medicine.

Some soldiers train US Army working dogs.

US COAST GUARD

The Coast Guard carries out law enforcement and defense duties near US shores. Founded in 1790, it was the first official department of the United States to protect US waters. Though the US Navy has its roots in the American Revolution, the Department of the Navy was not created until 1798. The modern Coast Guard and Navy share some duties in protecting US waters.

This painting shows what ships in the US Coast Guard looked like when it was founded.

Alexander Hamilton advocated for the creation of the Coast Guard. He believed the federal government needed to protect trade along its shores.

Unlike other US armed forces, the Coast Guard is a federal law enforcement agency as well as a military branch. At the recommendation of Secretary of the Treasury Alexander Hamilton, the US Congress created the Coast Guard to reduce smuggling, which was common at the time. The branch was originally known as the US Revenue-Marine. It was later renamed the US Revenue Cutter Service. It joined with the US Life-Saving Service to become the Coast Guard in 1915.

The Coast Guard today owns many of the lighthouses in the United States, including Pigeon Point Light Station in California.

A Coast Guard rescue swimmer was lowered to look for residents who had become stranded after the Red River flooded in North Dakota in 2009.

Over time, the Coast Guard has added more responsibilities. For example, it manages the country's lighthouses. These towers are equipped with a large, bright light that guides ships to the shore in darkness and difficult weather.

The Coast Guard also enforces laws that protect US fisheries and marine resources. Members of the Coast Guard stop vessels from bringing illegal drugs into the United States. The Coast Guard also performs safety inspections on civilian boats.

When accidents happen at sea, the Coast Guard typically leads the search for survivors. The Coast Guard helps sailors or passengers of sinking vessels. It also helps people if their planes go down over the ocean. The Coast Guard operates mainly from the water. But it also uses planes and helicopters

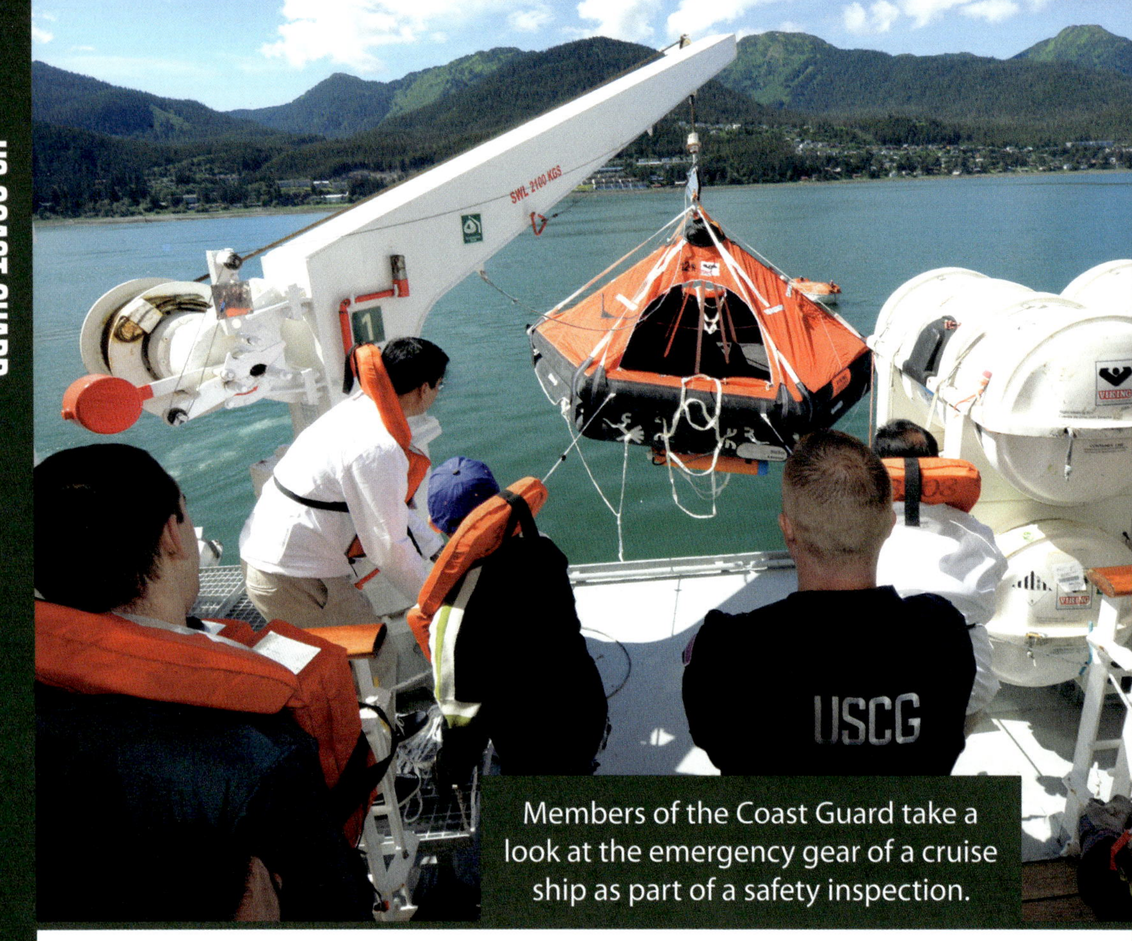

Members of the Coast Guard take a look at the emergency gear of a cruise ship as part of a safety inspection.

as part of its search-and-rescue duties. Today's Coast Guard even gathers information for the National Weather Service. This government agency provides weather forecasts for the entire United States.

Though both the Coast Guard and the Navy defend US waters, the two military branches have differences. The Coast Guard operates within and close to the United States, protecting its waterways and shorelines. The Navy sends its members all around the world. For this reason, the Coast Guard is a much smaller military branch than the Navy. It includes about 41,700 active-duty members and about 7,800 reservists.

The Navy has about 12 times more active-duty members than the Coast Guard.

The Coast Guard is the only branch of the US military that is under the authority of the Department of Homeland Security. Other military branches are supervised by the Department of Defense. During wartime, the US president has the power to transfer the Coast Guard to be under the supervision of the Department of the Navy, which falls under the Department of Defense.

Coast Guard pilots are able to pick up supplies without landing.

COAST GUARD SPECIAL FORCES

The Coast Guard has five special forces groups. Each group receives special training to carry out specific tasks at or near the US coastline. They may be responsible for responding to natural disasters or defending the United States against threats including terrorism.

The Maritime Safety and Security Teams (MSST) unit was created in 2002, one year after the terrorist attacks that took place in the United States on September 11, 2001. The main role of the MSST is to prevent terrorist attacks. The special operations unit guards US seaports and maritime facilities, which include docks, piers, and warehouses on the coast.

Maritime Safety and Security Teams patrol around Guantanamo Bay in Cuba, where there is a US military prison.

MSST members removed illegal drugs from a ship after disrupting a smuggling attempt in 2023.

Members take part in regular anti-terrorism training exercises. This helps ensure they will be prepared in the event of a terrorist attack against US facilities.

There are several types of MSST members. The Waterside Security Section enforces security zones. These are the areas surrounding maritime vessels or buildings where only authorized personnel are allowed. The Maritime Law Enforcement and Force Protection Team responds to threats, such as chemical or biological weapons, that may be aboard a ship or boat. In order to respond to these threats, MSST members must be able to quickly board and search suspicious vessels. They are trained to descend from a helicopter by rope onto a boat so they can perform searches at sea.

The Dive Team also makes up part of the MSST. Divers perform a variety of underwater security operations.

Some Coast Guard special forces train dogs to help with military operations. Dogs are able to detect explosives.

An MSRT practices an active-shooter drill aboard a ferry.

These include clearing obstructions from waterways and recovering weapons. There are even canine handling teams in the MSST. Canine handlers use dogs to sniff out dangerous devices, such as explosives.

The Maritime Security Response Team (MSRT) is an elite group that is trained in counterterrorism operations. While the MSST unit searches for potential threats, the MSRT responds if one is identified. Members of the MSRT receive extensive training in close-quarters combat. These skills are necessary for fighting enemies up close.

Port security units use maneuverable high-speed boats.

There are also specialized roles within the MSRT. For example, some members are trained to board vessels from small boats or helicopters. Other MSRT members observe from the air, land, or sea in case backup is needed. These MSRT members receive marksmanship training so they can defend their fellow team members from afar.

Port Security Units (PSUs) are also among the Coast Guard's special forces. They defend US ports and can be sent to respond to natural disasters. PSUs are trained to deploy quickly. PSUs are the only Coast Guard special operations units that are made up only of reservists. Each unit has 140 of these part-time Coast Guard members. There are eight PSUs in

MSRT members may need to quickly board a ship if it poses a threat to the United States.

TACLET members were called upon to help in Puerto Rico following Hurricane Maria in 2017.

the United States. Some are stationed along the Atlantic coast. Others are located on the Pacific coast or in the Gulf of Mexico. There is even a PSU stationed in Lake Erie in Ohio.

The Coast Guard's Tactical Law Enforcement Teams (TACLET) work to stop illegal drugs from being smuggled into the United States on boats. These teams are also trained to stop pirates from stealing goods from ships in US waters. When they are not dealing with crime, TACLET members train members of the navies and coast guards of other nations. This work helps strengthen alliances between those countries and the United States. It also helps limit smuggling of weapons and drugs around the world, making waterways safer for everyone.

The National Strike Force responds when hazardous materials are released into US waters. Sometimes these materials are released accidentally, such as an oil spill from a tanker. The National Strike Force is trained to deal with these kinds of environmental disasters. They are also trained to neutralize chemical and biological weapons that are released into US waters.

THE COAST GUARD IN THE WAR OF 1812

The Coast Guard has taken part in several wars. One such conflict was the War of 1812 (1812–1815). This war began in part because the United Kingdom was violating the maritime rights of the United States. The British Royal Navy sometimes illegally boarded US merchant ships it encountered at sea. The British sailors then tried to force the Americans on board to serve the British Navy. During this time, the Coast Guard was still called the Revenue-Marine.

Samuel Travis was the captain of a Revenue-Marine ship named the *Surveyor* during the War of 1812. The *Surveyor*

When dealing with hazardous materials, members of the National Strike Force need to wear protective gear.

The defense of the *Surveyor* showed the determination of US sailors against challenging odds.

was anchored at Gloucester Point, Virginia, on June 12, 1813. In the middle of the night, British soldiers prepared to take over the ship. They rowed small boats toward the *Surveyor*. Travis's crew spotted the British soldiers but were unable to angle their cannons to fire at the British. Travis instead armed his crew of about a dozen men with two muskets each. He told them to hold their fire until he gave his command. They waited in silence. The British did not know they had been spotted. Once the British entered range, Travis gave his order to start firing.

Sailors demonstrate pikes and fighting techniques used during the War of 1812.

The *Surveyor* crew did their best to keep their ship from being taken. But they were greatly outnumbered. Fifty British sailors climbed on board the ship. The crew of the *Surveyor* managed to kill three British sailors and wound seven before losing the battle. The Revenue-Marine proved to be much tougher than the British Navy expected. No members of the *Surveyor* were killed in the battle, but the British sailors took Travis's personal sword. The British captain later returned the sword to Travis as a sign of respect. He also sent a note describing his admiration for Travis's determination to protect the *Surveyor*.

Though the Battle of Gloucester Point did not end in US victory, Travis's crew demonstrated the values of the Revenue-Marine and the Coast Guard. They did not give up easily and fought bravely against their enemies. In 1927, the Coast Guard named one of its ships after Travis. It also named a building at its training center in Yorktown, Virginia, after Travis in 2015.

The US cutter *Vigilant*, *left*, stopped the *Dart*, *right*, a British ship that had captured approximately 20 US ships during the War of 1812.

The Coast Guard has approximately 1,900 cutters and boats. During the War of 1812, the United States had just 17 warships and 14 revenue cutters to face the British Navy's fleet of about 600 warships.

THE COAST GUARD IN THE SPANISH-AMERICAN WAR

The Spanish-American War (1898) broke out between the United States and Spain in April 1898. The war began when the United States supported Cuba's fight for independence against Spain. Spain had controlled the island of Cuba for centuries. Spain and the United States agreed to a cease-fire just a few months later in August.

Many of the battles took place on the waters surrounding Cuba. The US Navy and Revenue Cutter Service had created a blockade in the harbor to keep Spanish ships from reaching the island. A Spanish fleet attempted to break through the blockade but was unsuccessful. It turned and anchored near the Cuban city of Cárdenas. The US Navy sent ships to stop the Spanish fleet from trying again.

As the USS *Winslow* got closer, it came under enemy fire. The *Winslow* suffered heavy damage to its steering gear

The USS *Winslow* was a torpedo boat.

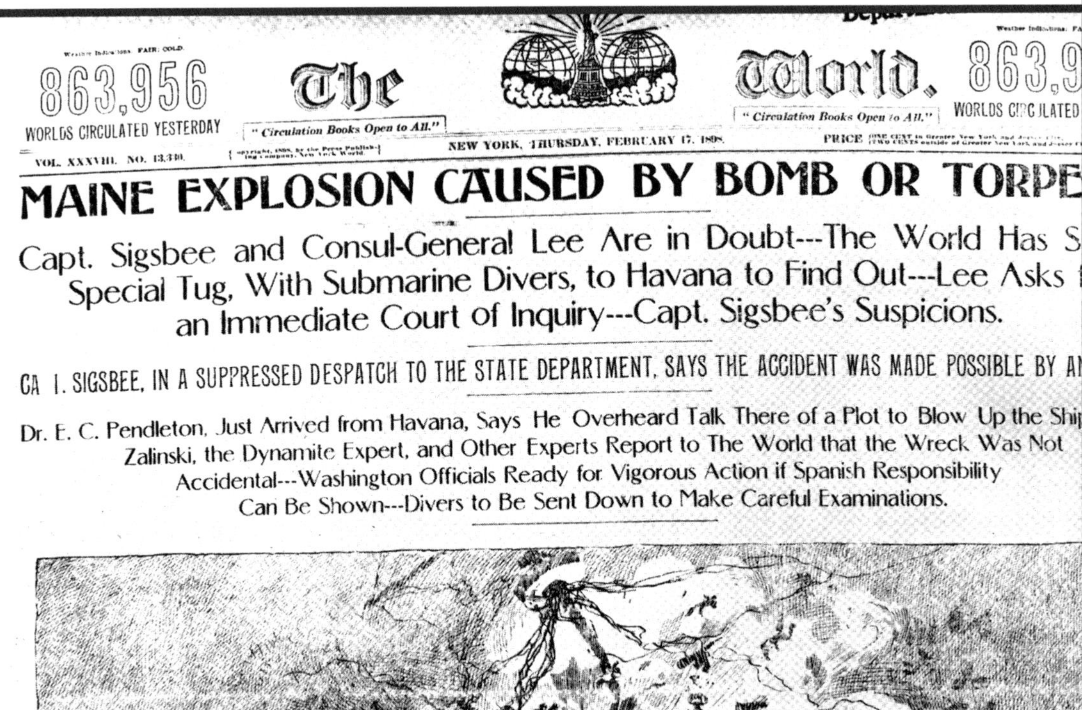

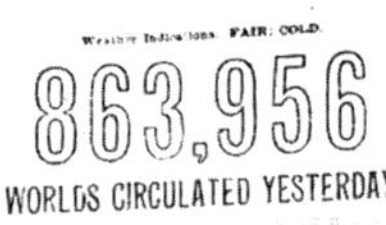

VOL. XXXVIII. NO. 13,330.

The

World.

" Circulation Books Open to All."

NEW YORK, THURSDAY, FEBRUARY 17, 1898.

863,9
WORLDS CIRCULATED

MAINE EXPLOSION CAUSED BY BOMB OR TORPE

Capt. Sigsbee and Consul-General Lee Are in Doubt---The World Has S Special Tug, With Submarine Divers, to Havana to Find Out---Lee Asks f an Immediate Court of Inquiry---Capt. Sigsbee's Suspicions.

CA I. SIGSBEE, IN A SUPPRESSED DESPATCH TO THE STATE DEPARTMENT, SAYS THE ACCIDENT WAS MADE POSSIBLE BY AI

Dr. E. C. Pendleton, Just Arrived from Havana, Says He Overheard Talk There of a Plot to Blow Up the Shi Zalinski, the Dynamite Expert, and Other Experts Report to The World that the Wreck Was Not Accidental---Washington Officials Ready for Vigorous Action if Spanish Responsibility Can Be Shown---Divers to Be Sent Down to Make Careful Examinations.

A New York newspaper reported on the explosion of the USS *Maine* in a Cuban harbor in 1898. This was one of the main causes of the Spanish-American War.

and engines. The *Hudson*, a Revenue Cutter ship, towed the *Winslow* to safety, saving many US lives. The *Hudson* crew received special medals from President William McKinley for their service that day.

THE COAST GUARD IN WORLD WAR II

Military members who show exceptional bravery are awarded medals. The US Congress has given out more than 3,500 Medals of Honor during the nation's history. But only one has been awarded to a member of the Coast Guard.

The US blockade of Cuba during the Spanish-American War eventually caused the Spanish to surrender some of their ports on the island.

The Tactical Coxswain Course prepares coxswains with the skills they need in order to react to high-risk situations.

Douglas Munro joined the Coast Guard in 1939, two years before the United States joined World War II. Munro trained as a coxswain for landing craft. In this position he drove small boats used to transport soldiers from larger ships onto enemy beaches. In August 1942, Munro and other coxswains took a group of Marines to the Solomon Islands in the southwestern Pacific Ocean. By late September, Munro's commanding officer had received word that the Marines they had dropped off were in trouble and being attacked by Japanese soldiers. The Marines needed to be pulled from the island quickly.

As the Coast Guard members approached the island, they came under fire. One coxswain did not think it would be possible to save the Marines. He told Munro to fall back. But Munro refused to abandon the Marines. He headed for the islands despite heavy gunfire from the Japanese soldiers. The Marines swam out to Munro's boat, which had been positioned to shield the US soldiers from bullets. During the rescue, a Coast Guard boat had gotten stuck on a nearby reef. When Munro saw it, he headed to it immediately. The Marines tied a rope to the vessel so Munro could free it.

The Japanese soldiers were still firing as the Marines and Coast Guard coxswains continued their escape. A fellow Coast Guard member noticed bullets splashing into

The Coast Guard used landing craft to carry soldiers during World War II.

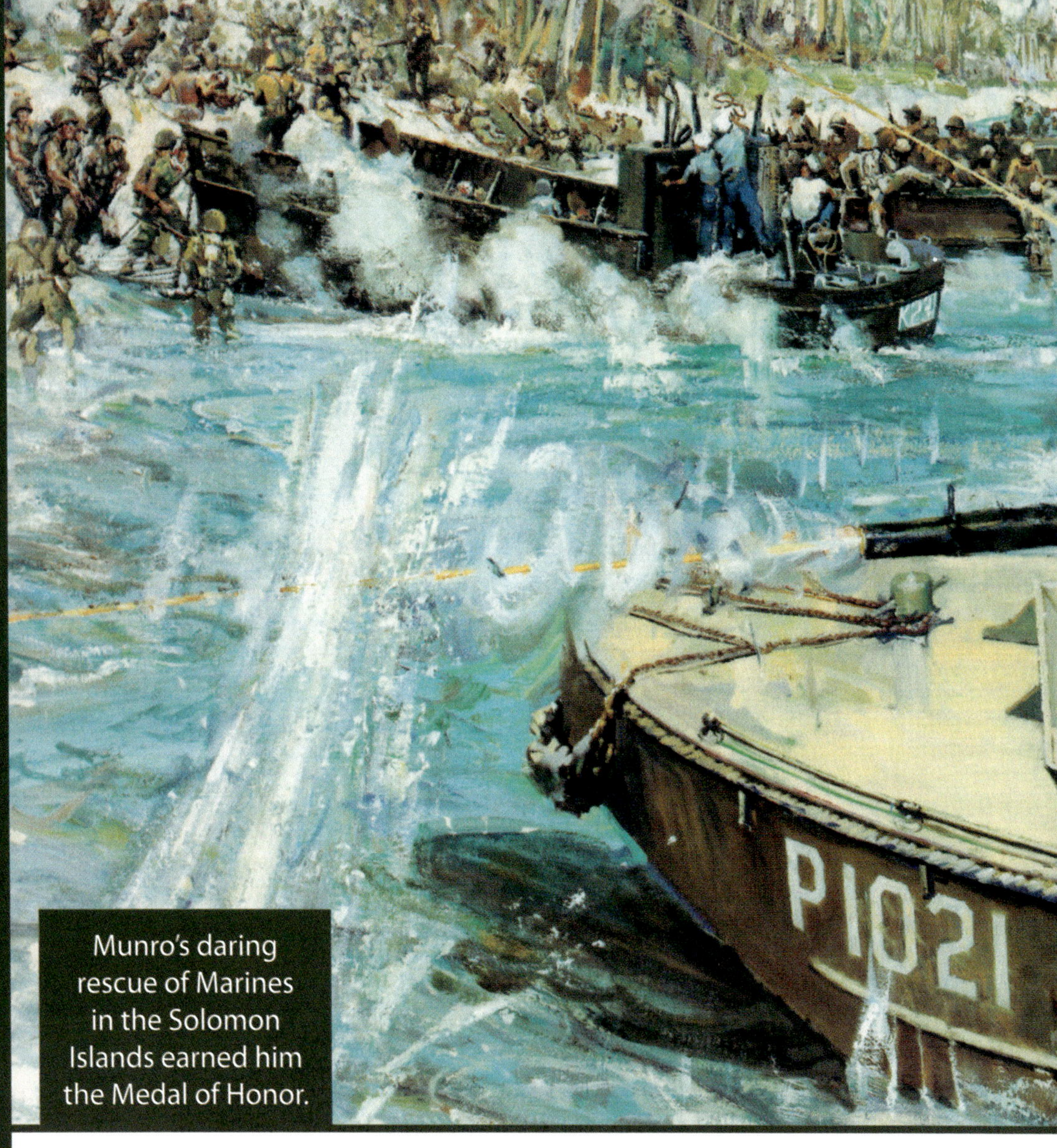

Munro's daring rescue of Marines in the Solomon Islands earned him the Medal of Honor.

the sea near their boat. He told Munro to get down, but the warning came too late. Munro had been hit. He saved the Marines on the beach. But he had given his own life for the success of his mission. The following May, President Franklin D. Roosevelt presented Munro's parents with their son's Medal of Honor.

WOMEN IN THE COAST GUARD

Women served as lighthouse keepers for the Lighthouse Service as early as the 1830s. This department later merged with the Coast Guard. Few women served in the Coast Guard or its predecessors in the 1800s or early 1900s.

The Coast Guard held a memorial service for Douglas Munro in 2013.

It wasn't until 1941 that the Coast Guard hired its first female civilian employee.

During World War II, Roosevelt signed a bill that created the Coast Guard Women's Reserve. This allowed women to serve as reservists for the Coast Guard. The division was nicknamed SPARS after the Latin phrase *Semper Paratus*. This motto of the Coast Guard means "Always Ready." While women were allowed to serve in the Coast Guard, their roles were limited. Most worked as radio and telephone operators.

At first, only white women were permitted to join SPARS. But in 1945, Olivia Hooker became the first Black woman to enlist in the Coast Guard. She worked at a separation center in Boston, Massachusetts, where she was responsible for discharging Coast Guard members at the end of their service. Hooker went on to earn a master's degree and

A member of the Coast Guard performs service work on the Craighill Channel lighthouse in Maryland.

More than 10,000 women volunteered to join SPARS between 1942 and 1946.

a doctorate in psychology after her military service ended. In 2015, Hooker attended a United States Coast Guard graduation ceremony as a guest. She was 100 years old at the time. Hooker sat in the front row as President Barack Obama gave a speech at the ceremony. Obama referred to Hooker as "an inspiration."

SPARS was disbanded when World War II ended, and women were once again left out of the US armed forces. In 1948, President Truman signed a bill allowing women to serve in all branches of the US military. At first, female Coast Guard members had to serve separately from men in a reserve division. Women finally joined an integrated Coast

After her time in the Coast Guard, Hooker provided therapy for children with learning disabilities for many years.

Guard and served alongside men starting in 1973. They were also allowed to serve as active-duty members as well as reservists.

In 2021, more than 5,800 women served as active members of the Coast Guard.

Coast Guard members receive regular training on water survival skills.

JOINING THE COAST GUARD

Applying to the Coast Guard starts with the same basic steps as joining other branches of the United States military. Applicants must take the ASVAB. High school graduates must score at least 40 on the AFQT section. GED holders need a minimum score of 50.

As with other military branches, new enlistees must attend basic training. For Coast Guard members, this program lasts for eight weeks. Basic training involves a wide range of physical fitness activities. But there is a focus on swimming skills. Even strong swimmers often need to work hard to pass the 12-minute swim test that is required of all Coast Guard members.

Most new enlistees enter the Coast Guard at the rank of seaman recruit (E-1). They can be promoted up to a master chief petty officer (E-9). New recruits can be commissioned as officers depending on their prior education and experience. But many people go through the Coast Guard Academy to become officers. At this school, people choose from a variety of majors including engineering, math,

Members of the Coast Guard practice towing techniques. They should be comfortable with the basics of boat handling.

Aviation Survival Technicians are a special class of Coast Guard Rescue Swimmers. They receive an additional 22 weeks of training that includes learning survival skills.

and science. Competition to get into this school is tough. Only 14 percent of applicants are accepted.

Coast Guard officer ranks begin with Ensign (O-1) and go all the way up to Admiral (O-10). Officers serve in a number of professions that require more education and training. For example, a Coast Guard officer may serve as a health care provider or a pilot.

The Coast Guard also includes civilian positions. People may perform a range of jobs including food preparation, mechanical maintenance, or diving. These people play important roles in carrying out the daily operations of the Coast Guard.

Coast Guard members perform routine maintenance of ships and boats to make sure systems are running smoothly.

US MARINE CORPS

Marines need to be prepared to travel across all types of terrain, including jungles and forests.

Army soldiers are trained to fight battles on land. Sailors in the Navy are trained for battles at sea. Members of the Marine Corps use many of the skills taught in the Army and Navy. Marines travel by sea and fight on land.

The Marine Corps was formed in November 1775 during the American Revolution. It was known as the Continental Marines. About four months later, the Marines headed for their first mission. They were led by Captain Samuel Nicholas, the first commissioned officer of the military branch. Nicholas and his Marines sailed to the port of Nassau in the Bahamas with members of the Continental Navy. The Bahamas were a British colony at the time. The Continental Marines and Continental

Navy raided the Bahamas for gunpowder and weapons that the British had stored there. A militia of about 110 people tried to defend the island town. But they were outnumbered by the 260 sailors and Marines who took victory in what is now known as the Battle of Nassau. When the war ended, the Continental Marines were disbanded.

President John Adams brought back the service as the US Marine Corps to protect US ships in 1798. In 1829, President Andrew Jackson tried to combine the Marine Corps with the Army. But Congress did not support Jackson's wishes. Instead, it passed the Act for the Better Organization of the United States Marine Corps in 1834.

Marines often use amphibious assault vehicles, which can operate on both land and water.

Marines practice moving from ship to shore.

This legislation kept the Marine Corps as its own branch of the military under the Department of the Navy. Today, the Marine Corps and Navy are thought of as sister branches of the armed forces. Both perform many of their duties at sea. But the Marine Corps specializes in moving from ship to shore regularly.

Marines are trained in offensive and defensive combat. They also gather intelligence, provide security, and assist in humanitarian missions. The Marine Corps protects US ships, military bases, and embassies around the world. Marines respond quickly to threats against the United States.

Marines use radio devices to communicate with aircraft and to coordinate activity.

The Marine Corps also employs many civilians. These people help repair military equipment and vehicles, provide health care, manage finances, and more.

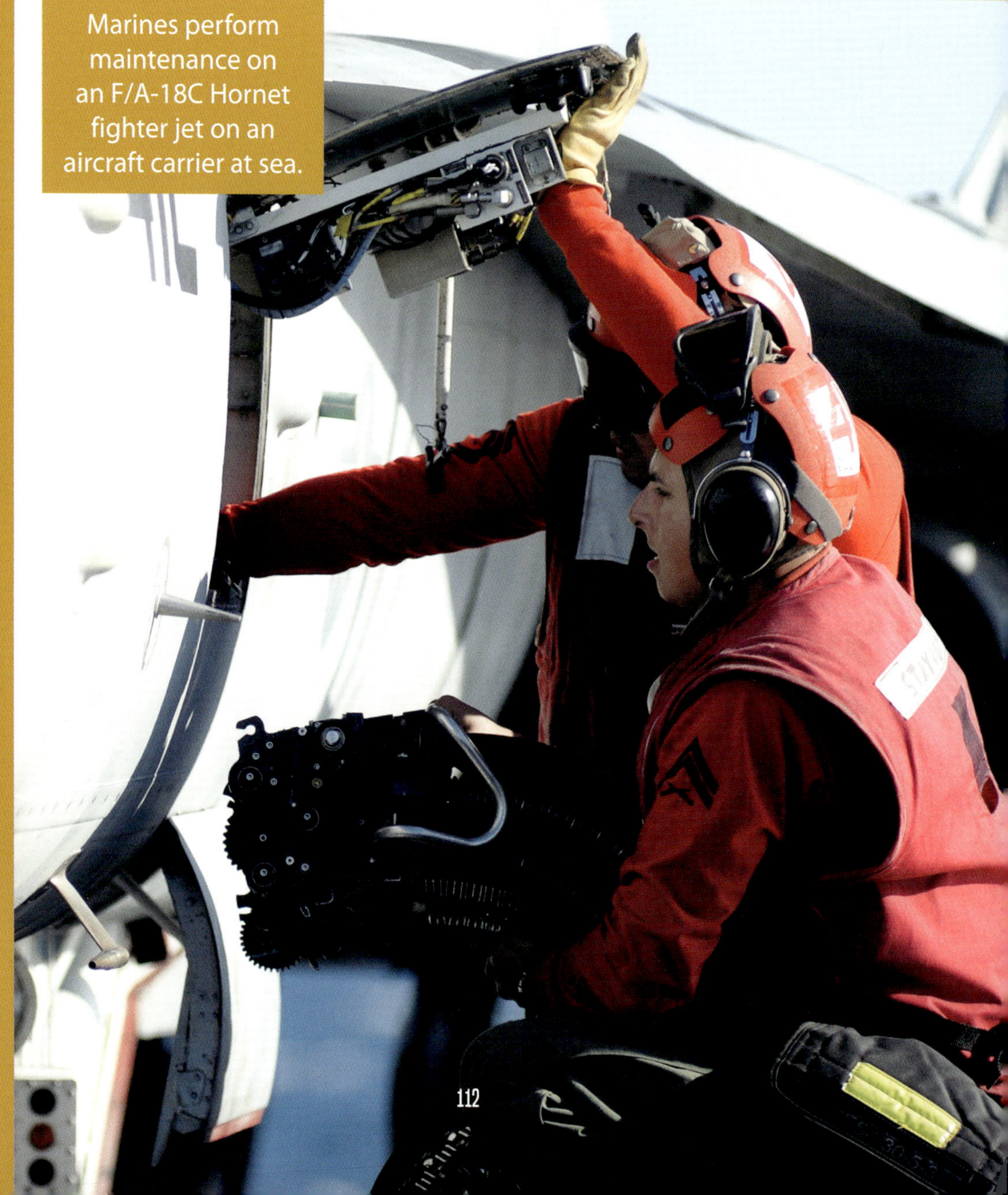

Marines perform maintenance on an F/A-18C Hornet fighter jet on an aircraft carrier at sea.

Reconnaissance and surveillance operations are often performed under the cover of night.

MARINE CORPS SPECIAL FORCES

The Marine Corps has two special forces groups. They are the Force Reconnaissance (RECON) and the Marine Raiders. Both groups receive extensive training to conduct some of the most dangerous missions in the US military. The US Marine Forces Special Operations Command (MARSOC) oversees these special operations groups.

Force RECON Marines are trained in combat, but often a successful Force RECON mission is one in which no combat takes place. Reconnaissance is a major responsibility of this special operations force. This type of work is typically done stealthily. Force RECON members are trained to collect information and get out of the area without attracting attention. They may swim and dive to reach enemy territory undetected. In addition to swimming, Force RECON Marines may need to run, jump, and climb on their missions. They are also trained to parachute from airplanes.

Marine Raiders also do reconnaissance work. But Marine

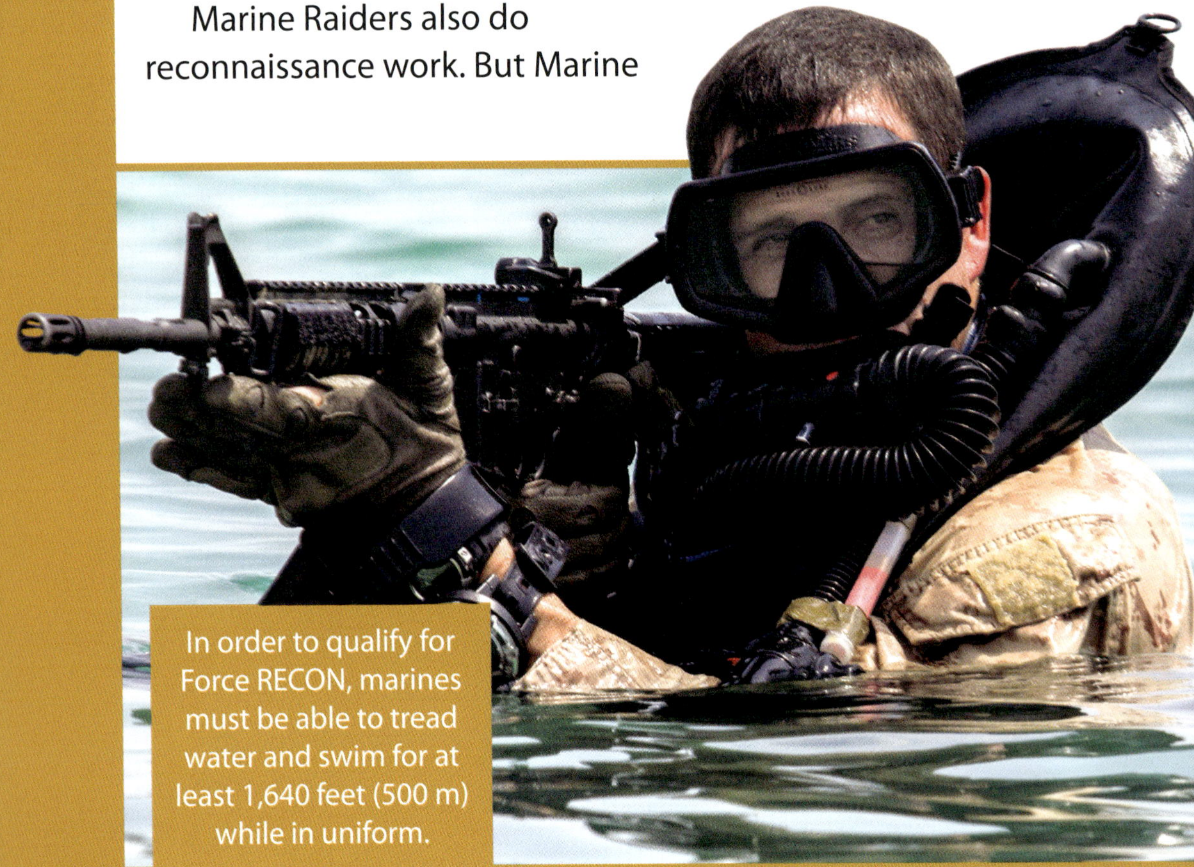

In order to qualify for Force RECON, marines must be able to tread water and swim for at least 1,640 feet (500 m) while in uniform.

Marine Raiders conduct practice raids to prepare for missions around the world.

Raiders primarily perform raids in enemy territory, which often requires offensive combat. These raids have many purposes. Marine Raiders may work to capture land, seize weapons, or recover allies. They may place mines or fire weapons to damage targets.

Marine Raiders have other responsibilities too. They help prevent and respond to terrorist attacks. They keep track of

Marine Raiders are sometimes required to parachute into dangerous territory.

weapons of mass destruction, such as nuclear bombs, and make sure those weapons are not threats to others. Marine Raiders sometimes work with foreign militaries. They may help an allied government stop insurgent forces. They can teach other militaries to defend themselves against rebel forces.

THE EARLY MARINE CORPS

In October 1803, the USS *Philadelphia* struck a reef off the coast of Tripoli in North Africa. The Navy ship and its crew were captured by pirates and taken ashore. The Navy sent Lieutenant Stephen Decatur to destroy the ship, preventing the pirates from using it. He and his crew arrived at the Tripoli harbor in February 1804 aboard the *Intrepid*, which was disguised to look like a local ship. They successfully burned the *Philadelphia*.

The modern Marine Corps practices reclaiming vessels that have been taken over by pirates.

Marines had to cross the desert to get into position in Derna. Members of the Marine Corps today may train in similar conditions.

The crew of the *Philadelphia* were still being held hostage by the pirates. The United States devised a strategy to free them. They planned to capture the city of Derna in present-day Libya, which was controlled by Tripoli. Capturing Derna would put pressure on the pirates to return the hostages. Led by Lieutenant Presley Neville O'Bannon of the Marine Corps, a small group of Marines were joined by about 400 allied soldiers from the region. They journeyed from Alexandria, Egypt, to Derna. They had to travel more than 500 miles (805 km) across the desert to reach the target location.

The Battle of Derna was successful, and the city was eventually captured by the United States. The United States paid for the release of the crew of the *Philadelphia*. The battle marked the first US land victory in a foreign country. Marines still sing about this victory in "The Marines' Hymn." The first verse includes the line "From the halls of Montezuma to the shores of Tripoli, we fight our country's battles in the air, on land, and sea."

The Navy ship USS *Tripoli* is named after the Marine Corps victory against Tripoli at Derna.

WOMEN IN THE MARINE CORPS

At first, only men were allowed to join the US military. During World War I, the Marine Corps and other military branches allowed women to join their ranks. Opha May Johnson became the first woman in the Marine Corps on August 13, 1918. The typed enlistment papers referred to the person enrolling as a man and used only pronouns such as *he* and *him*. The recruiting officer crossed out these pronouns and replaced them with *she* and *her* on Johnson's form.

Johnson worked as a clerk, typing and performing other office duties. Her time in the service was short. World War I ended 90 days after her enlistment. But she helped pave the way for many other women who joined the Marine Corps after her. In 1943, Captain Anne Lentz became the first female commissioned Marine officer. In 1978, Brigadier General Margaret Brewer became the first female Marine general. And in 2018, Marina Hierl became the first female Marine to lead an infantry platoon.

Following her service in World War I, Opha May Johnson worked as a clerk in the US Department of War.

In 2018, less than 9 percent of US Marines were women.

THE MARINE CORPS IN WORLD WAR II

One of the bloodiest World War II battles took place on the Japanese island of Iwo Jima. Approximately 80,000 Marines were sent to take the island in February 1945. The United States was interested in using the island as an emergency landing site for bomber planes.

Marines lie behind a hill on the beaches of Iwo Jima in 1945 to protect themselves from Japanese artillery.

Iwo Jima belonged to the United States from 1945 to 1968, when the island was returned to Japan.

Iwo Jima is a small island, with an area of just 8 square miles (21 sq km). But its mountainous terrain made the mission especially difficult. Making it to the top of Mount Suribachi was a key step for the Marines. Taking control of the highest ground would make it possible to see enemies in all directions. Capturing Mount Suribachi would make it easier for the United States to take control of the island. It took Marines several days to reach the summit.

After 32 more days, the United States controlled the rest of the island. More than 7,000 Marines were killed as the fight raged on. Another 20,000 Marines were wounded. But the

Japanese losses were even greater. About 20,000 Japanese troops fought in the battle. Only about 200 of them survived.

The Navajo Code Talkers played a major role in the Marine Corps' success at Iwo Jima. Members of the armed forces sometimes used codes to communicate plans with one another. Enemy soldiers could intercept the coded message, but they would not be able to understand its contents. In order to ensure that the enemy would not be able to read its messages, the US military used complex codes.

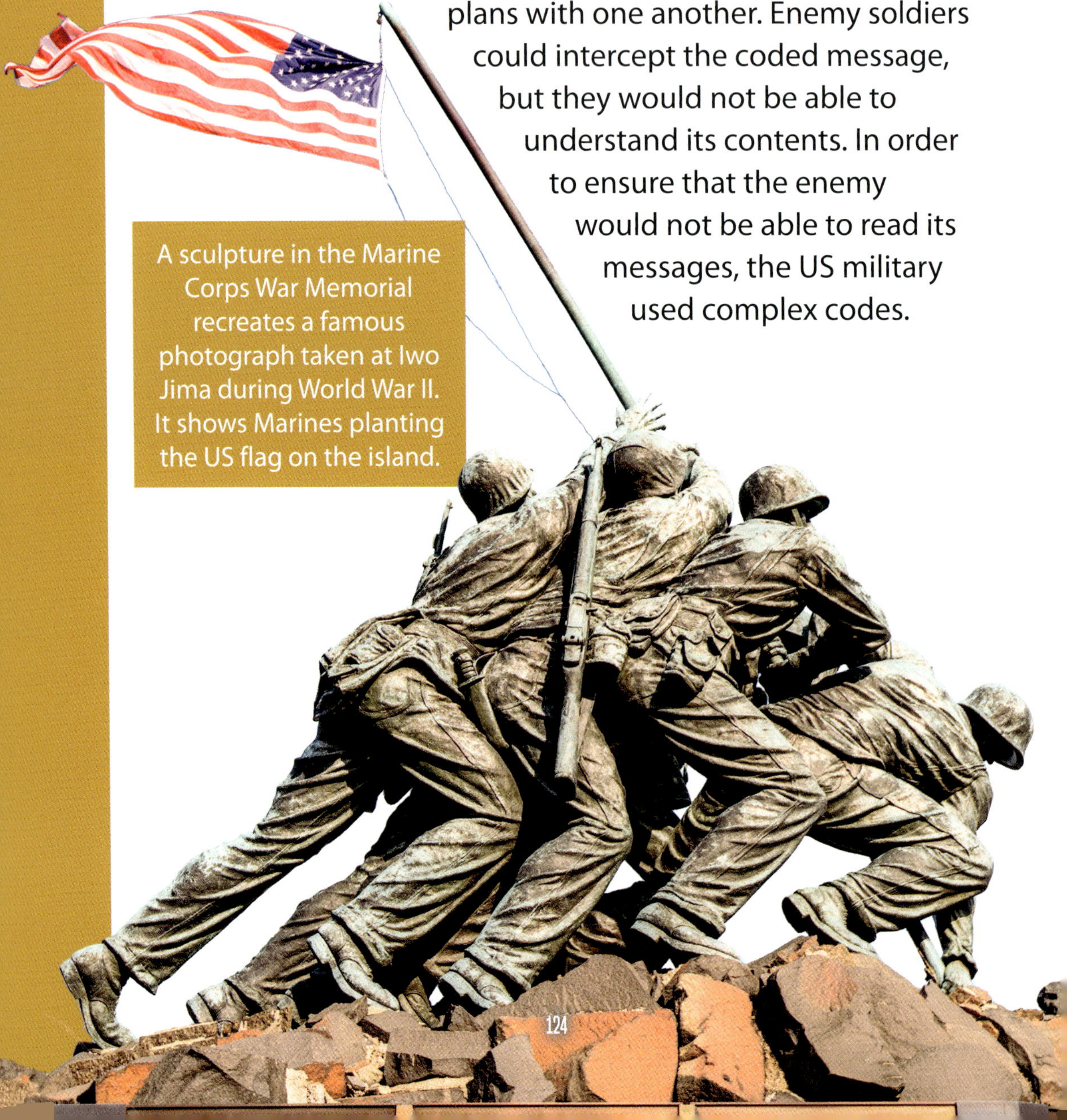

A sculpture in the Marine Corps War Memorial recreates a famous photograph taken at Iwo Jima during World War II. It shows Marines planting the US flag on the island.

The Navajo Code Talkers played a major role in the victory at Iwo Jima.

Even with code-breaking machines, it could take a long time to decipher a message. The Marines wanted a faster solution. US marine Philip Johnston suggested enlisting Diné people from the Navajo Reservation to help.

The Navajo language is largely unwritten. It was unlikely to be understood by enemies. The Marine Corps recruited 29 Diné men to serve as Code Talkers. The Navajo Code Talkers used two types of code. In the first type, Navajo terms represented

The Navajo Code Talkers used the code word *lo-tso* to talk about battleships. *Lo-tso* directly translates to "whale."

letters of the English alphabet. For example, the Navajo word *wo-la-chee* translates to "ant." *Wo-la-chee* represented the letter *A*. In the second type of code, the Code Talkers created phrases in their language that would represent key military terms. Many words did not have a prior translation in the Navajo language. One example is the word *submarine*. The Code Talkers decided to call these vehicles *besh-lo*, which directly translates to "iron fish."

With the help of the Code Talkers, Marines were able to communicate much more quickly with one another. It had taken code-breaking machines 30 minutes to decipher three lines of code, whereas the Code Talkers could translate the same code in 20 seconds. During the Battle of Iwo Jima, six Code Talkers transmitted more than 800 messages to help ensure a US victory.

Navajo Code Talkers were honored before a Major League Baseball game between the Los Angeles Dodgers and Arizona Diamondbacks in 2015.

JOINING THE MARINE CORPS

The requirements to join the US Marine Corps are similar to those of the other military branches. Applicants with a high school diploma must score a minimum of 31 on the AFQT section of the ASVAB. A score of 50 is required for those with a GED. But the training involved in this branch of the military is

A Marine carries another soldier during training. This action may be necessary if an ally is wounded in combat.

During boot camp, Marine Corps recruits learn how to work together in small teams to complete missions.

especially demanding. Marine boot camp is often said to be the hardest basic training of all the military branches.

Marine Corps boot camp lasts for 13 weeks. Training is broken into three phases. The first four weeks include physical training, martial arts, and first aid. New recruits also learn about the history of the Marine Corps during this time. The second phase, which lasts five weeks, teaches additional combat skills and marksmanship. The final four-week phase includes working on swimming skills and operating military vehicles.

The third phase of boot camp also includes a challenging test known as the Crucible. This test pushes recruits to their physical limits. They are required to hike for 48 miles (77 km)

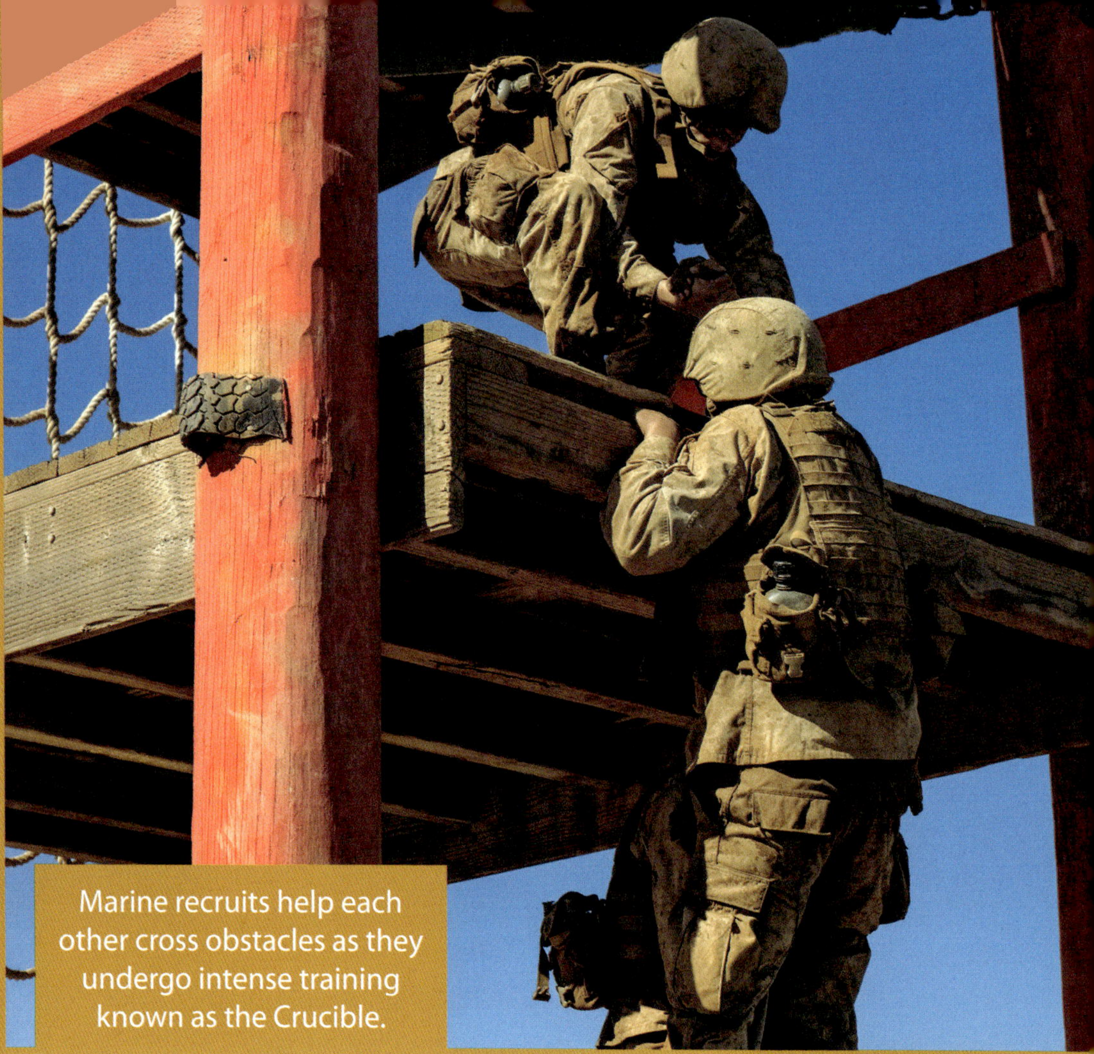

Marine recruits help each other cross obstacles as they undergo intense training known as the Crucible.

while carrying more than 40 pounds (18 kg) of gear. They are also challenged mentally. Recruits must prove they can work as a team and continue onward even when they are tired and have limited food. The Crucible lasts for 54 hours and includes several training and team-building events.

While attending boot camp, new recruits do not have a rank. Following graduation,

most new Marines enter as privates (E-1). They can then earn promotions up to sergeant major (E-9).

The process of becoming an officer in the Marine Corps is similar to the process in other branches. Graduates of the US Naval Academy enter the force as officers. College graduates who have completed the Naval ROTC program become officers too. People may choose to attend a Platoon Leaders Class when they are undergraduate students. This summer course prepares

The Combat Course prepares officer trainees for combat conditions in various environments.

Marines may specialize in intelligence and communication systems. These skills help Marine Corps units communicate with one another and with other branches of the armed forces.

college students to be officers in the Marine Corps. College seniors and graduates who did not go through ROTC must apply to and attend the Officer Candidate Course. They become officers after completing this ten-week program. Officers start as second lieutenants (O-1) and can advance all the way to the rank of general (O-10).

Marines can choose from many types of careers within the corps. They may become part of the infantry. These ground forces are what many people think of when they picture a Marine. It takes a lot of physical and mental toughness to serve in the infantry.

Marines are not limited to combat positions. Marines working in intelligence gather and handle classified information. Logistics members help plan and manage military operations. Administrators handle paperwork. They may deal with everything from filing papers to preparing items for postal delivery. Civilians working for the Marine Corps might also specialize in intelligence, logistics, or administration.

People working in administrative roles in the Marine Corps make sure that daily operations run smoothly.

US NAVY

The earliest version of the US Navy was formed in the late 1700s before the United States was an independent country. The British had forbidden the colonists from trading with other nations without permission. But to win independence, the Americans needed many supplies for the war. They were unable to produce all the supplies they would need on their

The British Navy had many more ships than the Continental Navy. But the colonists were still able to win battles at sea, such as when they took supplies from the Bahamas, which was a British colony.

The Continental Navy had only around 20 ships during the American Revolution. In 2022, the Navy had more than 280 ships, the second-most of any nation behind China.

own. Some could be obtained by trade or by seizing them from British ships. But the colonists would need a strong fleet of ships to accomplish these tasks. The fleet would protect cargo ships as they sailed along the Atlantic coast for trade. It also needed to be strong enough to face the powerful British navy.

The colony of Rhode Island sent delegates to the Continental Congress in Philadelphia in August 1775. They were the first to suggest a navy. They asked for a fleet of ships to be dedicated to protecting American ports as the colonies

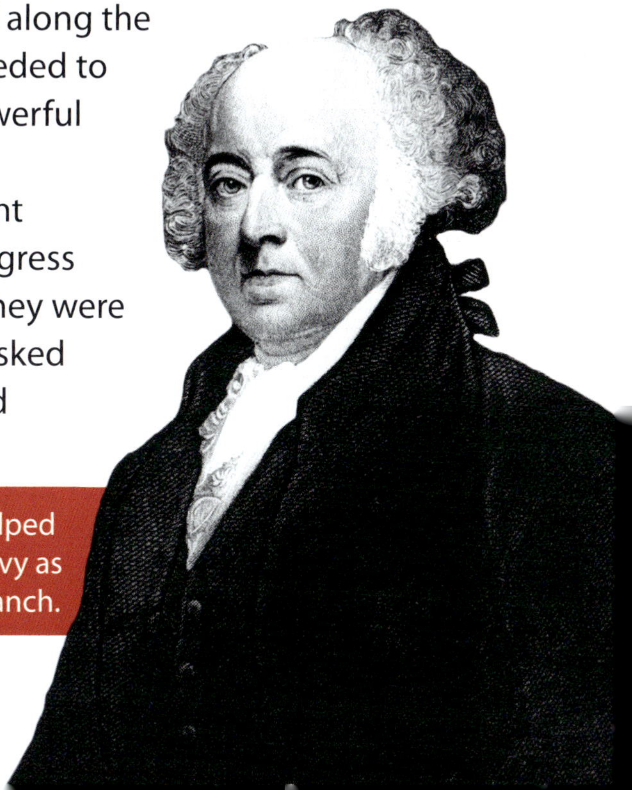

John Adams helped establish the Navy as a US military branch.

The Navy is responsible for protecting US interests at sea.

prepared for war. By October, the Continental Congress had agreed to provide the fleet.

The Navy was in service throughout the American Revolution, but it was not maintained after the war ended. It became apparent that the new nation needed a permanent naval force by the time John Adams became president of the United States in 1797. He worked with Congress to make the Navy an official branch of the military before the United States entered the Quasi-War (1798–1801).

This conflict started because the French and the British were at war with each other. The United States had wanted to remain neutral. It was a new country and wanted to establish trade with both nations. France was angry with this decision. It had

Some Navy sailors are trained to fire machine guns from helicopters.

Navy sailors train to respond in case of aircraft emergencies.

assisted the United States in the American Revolution and felt betrayed. France believed that the United States was helping its enemy by continuing to trade with the British. In response, France captured US merchant ships in the Atlantic Ocean. The United States built up its naval forces in response.

Since that time, the Navy has defended the United States in numerous wars and conflicts around the globe. The nation depends on this military branch to protect the country at sea. The Navy trains sailors so they are prepared for war. It also ensures that ships can safely transport goods around the world. In 2021, the US Navy had more than 343,000 active members.

Navy ships patrol the open ocean, and submarines travel under the surface. Other Navy vessels are equipped to navigate rivers. The Navy also operates aircraft, such as cargo planes, helicopters, and fighter jets. In fact, the US Navy has one of the largest aviation forces in the world, with 3,700 aircraft. It is second only to the US Air Force, which has more than 5,300 aircraft. Navy pilots are trained to land on aircraft carriers at sea.

It takes many sailors in a wide variety of roles for the Navy to carry out its many missions around the globe.

JOBS IN THE NAVY

There are many kinds of jobs available in the US Navy. Sailors work on ships, in the air, and on land. Some even dive below the waves to complete their missions. The work of all these sailors contributes to the overall success of the Navy.

Aviation Rescue Swimmers take part in rescues and humanitarian missions. These Navy personnel are skilled swimmers. They travel by helicopter to reach people in need of rescue. Sometimes, the people in trouble are military personnel. Aviation Rescue members also help civilians, such as refugees or victims on sinking watercraft. Aviation Rescue Swimmers must perform in challenging environments to provide emergency service. The people who need their help may be stuck in swift waters, high seas, or even sea caves.

Intense training strengthens special forces members physically and mentally.

Aviation Rescue Swimmers are responsible for getting wounded soldiers onto helicopters so that they can be taken to hospital ships.

The men and women in this role train for two years. During this time, they learn advanced swimming and lifesaving techniques. They must pass courses in helicopter mission equipment and helicopter weapons. Additionally, they learn survival skills for both water and land.

Aviation Rescue Swimmers may be assigned out at sea or near the shore. A sea assignment may be aboard an aircraft carrier, a support ship, or a surface combat ship. Aviation Rescue Swimmers with land assignments serve around the world.

Seabees are a unit of the Navy that specializes in construction. Along with other members of the Navy, Seabees may be sent to areas to offer humanitarian assistance.

Becoming an Aviation Rescue Swimmer requires extensive training in survival skills and search-and-rescue techniques.

The Explosive Ordnance Disposal group is the Navy's bomb squad. These technicians learn how to disable deadly explosive devices to keep them from harming US military members and allies. For example, there may be underwater mines that would damage ships and submarines if they exploded. Explosive Ordnance Disposal Technicians are responsible for disarming these mines so vessels can safely travel through waterways.

Explosive Ordnance Disposal Technicians operate in extremely stressful conditions. They must think quickly and remain calm in dangerous situations. They also need physical stamina for the job. Reaching an underwater mine is challenging. Ships cannot sail close to the explosive device, so technicians often need to jump out of airplanes and dive underwater. They wear heavy bomb suits while they work, even

Explosive Ordnance Disposal Technicians spend 42 weeks learning how to defuse different types of explosives, including bombs, missiles, and torpedoes.

when underwater. This protective clothing weighs about 70 pounds (32 kg). Technicians use advanced technology, such as robotic devices that help them examine and move explosives from a safer distance.

Navy Divers learn how to perform a variety of tasks beneath the ocean's surface. Some divers do repair work, such as welding, on ships. They may clear large debris so Navy vessels can move through previously

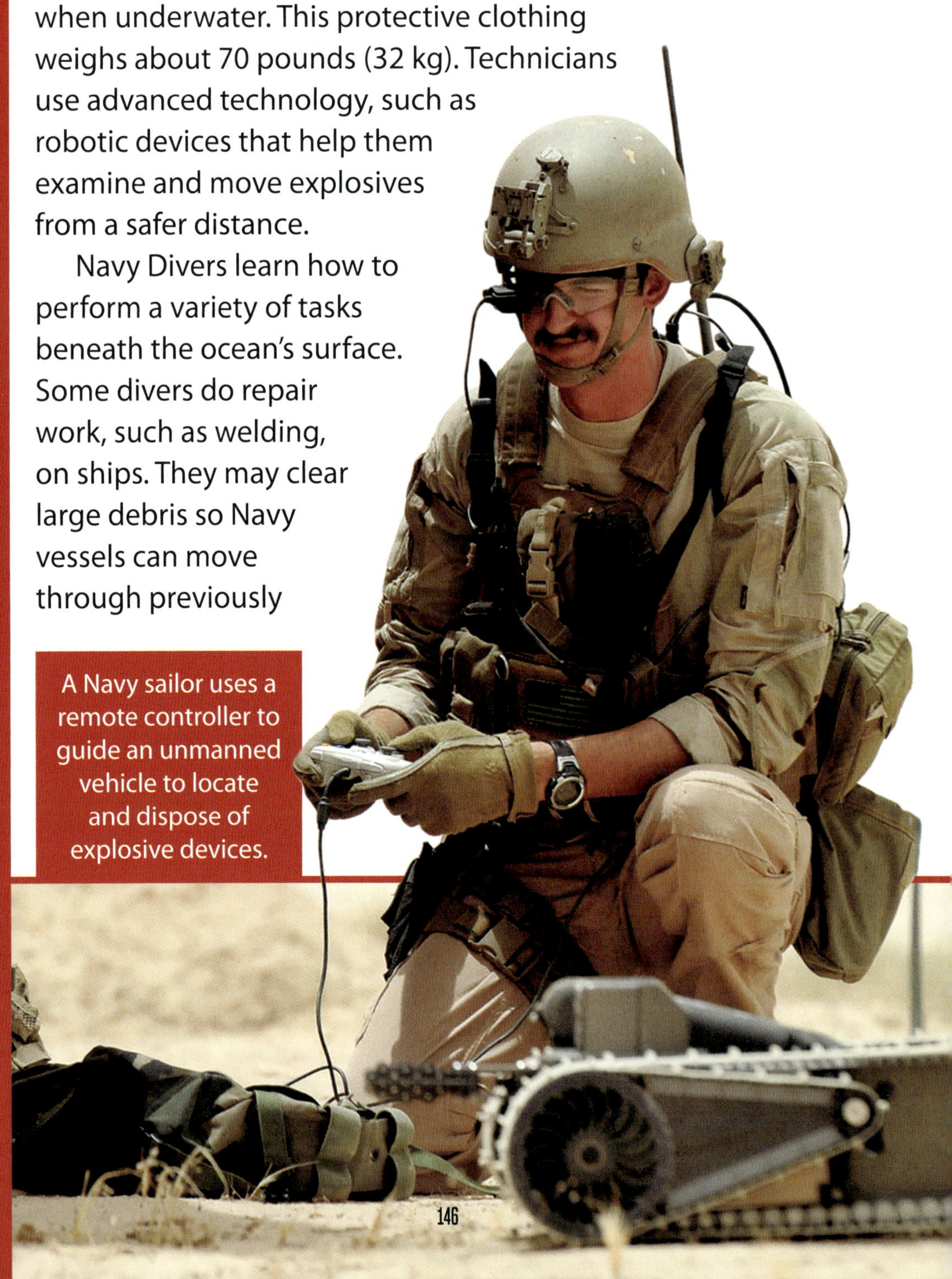

A Navy sailor uses a remote controller to guide an unmanned vehicle to locate and dispose of explosive devices.

Navy Divers may use a diver propulsion device (DPD) to help them travel quickly and stealthily underwater. Each DPD can carry two people.

blocked waterways. Other divers perform search-and-rescue work when sailors or pilots go missing. Navy Divers may bring wreckage from sea disasters up from the ocean floor. Some Navy Divers help astronauts who have just returned to Earth from a mission in space. When space capsules splash down in a body of water, Navy Divers retrieve the astronauts inside.

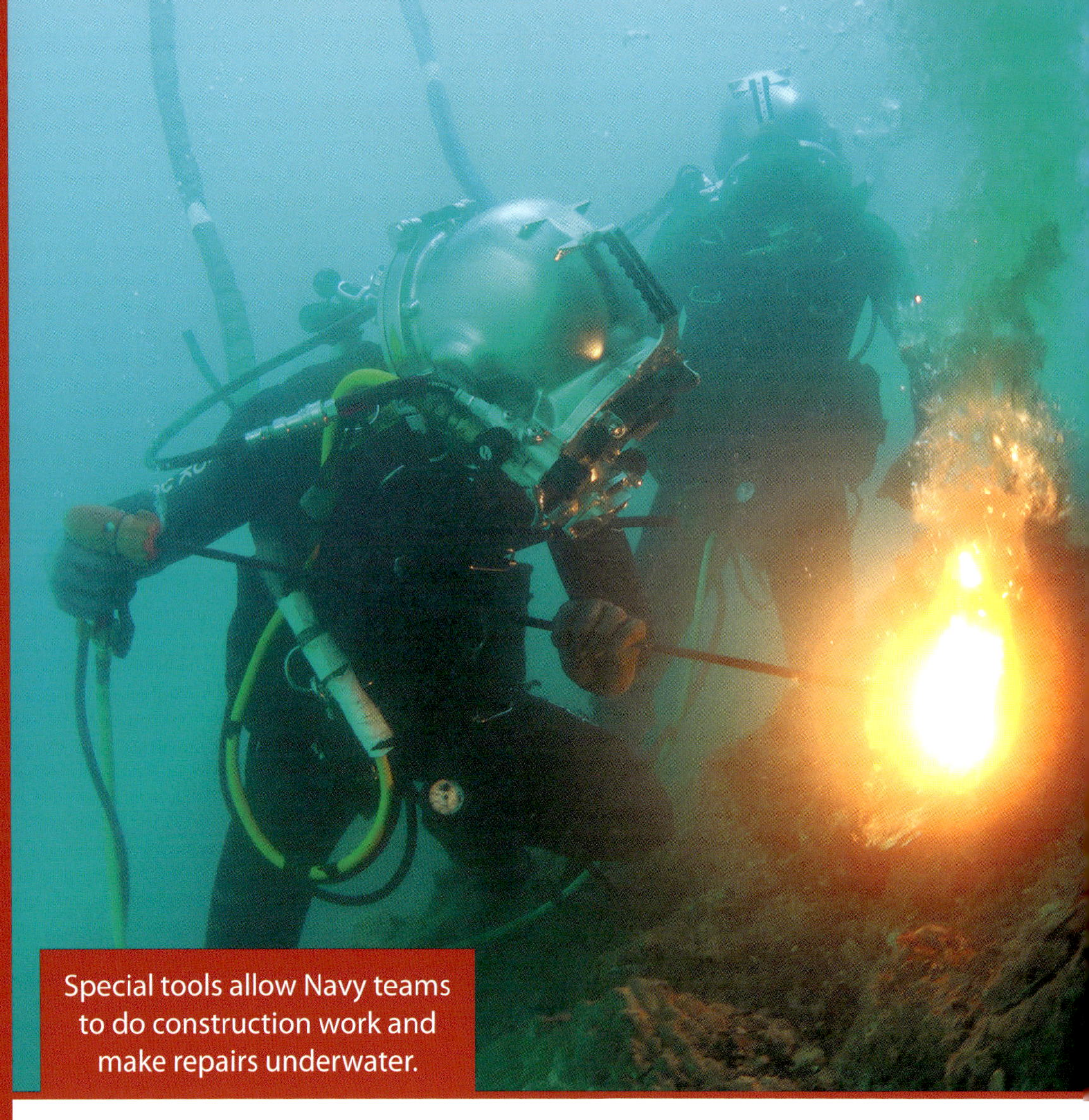

Special tools allow Navy teams to do construction work and make repairs underwater.

NAVY SPECIAL FORCES

Some of the most elite special forces groups are part of the Navy. Military members who want to join one of these groups must go through intense physical and mental training. Their work is both dangerous and difficult.

One of the most well-known special forces groups in the US military is the Navy SEALs. The letters stand for sea, air, and land because SEAL missions can take place in all of these locations. SEAL team members must be mature, self-confident, and able to work under extremely stressful conditions. SEALs are known for carrying out some of the most secret and dangerous missions for the United States.

The qualifications to become a Navy SEAL are extremely difficult to meet. Only a few people possess the skills and other qualities demanded of this special forces group. SEALs must be in top physical condition. They must complete a 500-yard (457 m) swim in less than 12 minutes and 30 seconds. Ideally, the Navy wants SEALs with times closer to 8 minutes. SEALs must also have high physical and mental endurance. SEAL missions often last for long periods with little to no opportunity for rest. SEALs must be able to continue performing at a high level even when their bodies and minds are tired.

SEALs are sent on a variety of covert missions. They may need to gather important

Navy SEALs receive more than two years of training before they are ready for missions.

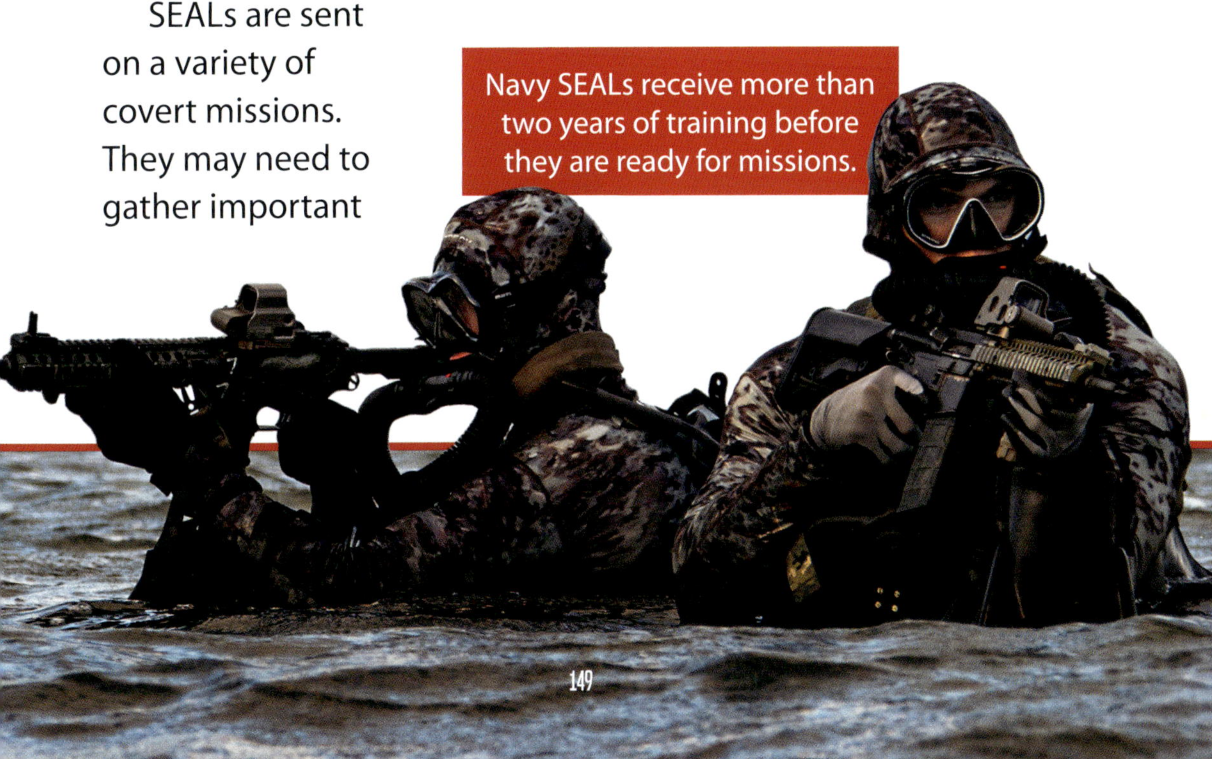

information that other military members are not equipped to uncover. They may need to destroy obstacles to help other military units accomplish their missions. They are called on to capture or kill key targets, such as terrorists. In 2011, SEAL Team 6 raided the compound in Pakistan where Osama bin Laden was hiding. Bin Laden was the head of the terrorist group

Navy SEALs must prepare for deployment in wintery and Arctic conditions.

Special Warfare Combatant-Craft Crewmen are trained to undertake reconnaissance missions in dangerous areas.

al-Qaeda, which claimed responsibility for the September 11, 2001, attacks on the United States. The operation was successful, and SEAL Team 6 killed bin Laden.

Special Warfare Combatant-Craft Crewmen are another special operations force of the Navy. They specialize in combat and reconnaissance in rivers and along coastlines. They may help transport Navy SEALs and other special forces troops. They may be tasked with locating and raiding enemy ships.

Navy sailors practice parachuting and landing techniques as part of special forces training.

Like other special forces groups of the US Navy, Special Warfare Combatant-Craft Crewmen require a great deal of training. They are highly trained in water skills, boat handling, and weapons skills. They must be ready to fight their way out of dangerous situations. They gather information about their enemies that can help other special forces groups.

THE NAVY IN WORLD WAR II

The Navy played a major role in battles in the Pacific Ocean during World War II. It secured a major victory at Midway, where a US military base was located. Japan wanted to take over this island, which would have secured its power in the Pacific. However, members of the US Navy had cracked the codes Japan had been using to communicate. They knew an attack on Midway was coming, and they were able to prepare for it.

Torpedo bombers waited on the deck of the USS *Enterprise* during preparations for the Battle of Midway.

The largest aircraft carriers used by the modern Navy can hold about 75 aircraft.

When Japanese aircraft carriers launched planes to bomb Midway, the US Navy was ready. The Navy used its own carriers to launch aircraft that attacked the Japanese fleet, sinking multiple vital carriers. Japan lost the Battle of Midway and was forced to retreat. This was a turning point in World War II and put the United States in position for victory.

Aircraft carriers remain important vessels in the modern Navy. These ships can be more than 1,000 feet (305 m) long, allowing aircraft to land on and take off from them. US aircraft carriers are powered by nuclear reactors, advanced sources of energy that can run for years before refueling. Carriers have been the backbone of US naval power for many decades.

A guided missile is launched from an aircraft carrier during a training exercise. The United States made advancements in guided missile technology following World War II.

Navy officers laid a wreath of flowers on the grave of Loretta Perfectus Walsh in 2011.

FAMOUS MEMBERS OF THE NAVY

The first women to serve in the Navy worked as nurses. Loretta Perfectus Walsh made history when she was sworn into the Navy in 1917. She became the first woman to serve in the armed forces in a nonnursing position. She served as a clerk. By 1941, more than 11,000 women were working in the Navy, mostly as nurses.

Some members of the Navy have achieved fame following their naval careers. Neil Armstrong started working toward a degree in aeronautical engineering under the Holloway Program Scholarship in 1947. This program required him to serve at least three years in the Navy. Armstrong's naval service took him to Asia to fight in South Korea in the Korean War. He flew

Neil Armstrong flew experimental planes after his Navy career.

Neil Armstrong received three Air Medals, *pictured*, and a Korean Service Medal for his role in the Korean War.

78 missions as a naval aviator. He received three Air Medals and survived being shot down in his F-9F Panther jet. Following his military career, Armstrong joined the US space program. Today, he is best known for being the first person to walk on the moon.

John F. Kennedy served in the Navy before becoming US president. He fought in World War II as a patrol torpedo boat commander and returned to the United States with multiple medals. These included a Purple Heart. He was the first US president to receive this medal.

As president, Kennedy relied on the Navy to help resolve the Cuban Missile Crisis. In October 1962, the United States learned that the Soviet Union was placing nuclear missiles in Cuba. The US government was concerned that the Soviets might attack the United States with these weapons. Kennedy demanded that the Soviets shut down the facilities. He called on the Navy. The military branch positioned ships to block Soviet vessels from delivering weapons to the island. For nearly two weeks, the world watched as a nuclear war seemed a possibility. But the crisis ended peacefully. On October 28, 1962, Soviet leader Nikita Khrushchev agreed to remove the weapons.

The USS *Joseph P. Kennedy, Jr.*, named for President Kennedy's older brother, was one of the ships that blocked shipments to Cuba.

JOINING THE NAVY

Joining the Navy begins with taking the ASVAB. This test helps identify the roles within the Navy that a person is best suited for. To join this military branch, applicants need a minimum score of 31 on the AFQT section of the ASVAB.

Navy boot camp lasts eight weeks. Like the basic training of other military branches, it includes a focus on physical fitness. Recruits will be tested on how quickly they can run 1.5 miles (2.4 km), the number of push-ups they can do in two minutes,

By the end of Navy boot camp, male recruits must be able to run 1.5 miles (2.4 km) in 16 minutes and 10 seconds. Female recruits must complete the run within 18 minutes and 37 seconds.

As part of basic training, Navy recruits learn first aid skills and prepare to respond to emergencies.

and how long they can hold a plank position. The Navy also has a rigorous swim test. Because members of the Navy will spend time at sea, they must be able to swim and stay afloat if they find themselves overboard. Recruits will be tested on different swim strokes, including the crawl stroke, backstroke, and sidestroke. Recruits also learn the basics of living and working on a ship during boot camp.

Enlisted navy members begin with the rank of seaman recruit (E-1) and can go up to the rank of master chief petty officer (E-9). Officer ranks start with ensign (O-1) and end with the rank of admiral (O-10).

In order to be a pilot for the Navy, one must be an officer.

Some people who want to become officers in the Navy attend Officer Candidate School (OCS). This is a 12-week program that trains people in the leadership skills to be naval officers. People also learn about naval warfare and military law while attending OCS. Graduates from the US Naval Academy and people who have completed Navy ROTC training can also enter the Navy as officers.

Some new officers go to Officer Development School (ODS) to learn additional skills. ODS is required for officers who are

Some Navy sailors receive advanced training in handling small watercraft.

Navy mechanics are responsible for repairing engines, brakes, steering systems, and more.

working in specialized fields, including engineering and health care. ODS lasts for five weeks and includes academic and physical training.

In addition to roles in the military, the Navy also employs civilians. People working in all kinds of fields can work for the Navy. Mechanics make sure that aircraft and ships are operating smoothly. Doctors keep people healthy. Scientists may perform research on fuel sources to make sure vehicles run as efficiently as possible. Information technology specialists and mathematicians can also find work within the Navy.

Scientists in the Navy perform experiments to understand how the body reacts to altitude changes.

US SPACE FORCE

President Donald Trump, *front*, signed the National Defense Authorization Act in 2019, which created the Space Force.

The US Space Force is the newest branch of the US military. It was formed on December 20, 2019, under President Donald Trump. The Space Force was created to protect the interests of the United States and other nations in outer space. Members of the Space Force are called Guardians. They protect spacecraft and make sure access to space is fair and safe.

The need for the Space Force arose because of the increasing importance of space technology for national security. US interest in space spiked in the 1950s, when the

United States entered a period of competition called the Space Race with the Soviet Union. Each country wanted to prove its superiority over the other by making advances in space technology. They began by launching satellites that would orbit Earth. The Soviet Union accomplished this task with *Sputnik* in 1957. The United States followed with *Explorer I* in 1958. Later that year, the National Aeronautics and Space Administration (NASA) was formed as the US space agency.

The Soviet Union was also the first nation to send a human to space. Cosmonaut Yuri Gagarin orbited Earth a single time in 1961. His entire trip lasted about 108 minutes. US astronaut

Chief Master Sergeant Roger Towberman of the Space Force unveiled the official flag of the Space Force on May 15, 2020.

John Glenn became the first American to accomplish this task nearly one year later. His trip included three full orbits of the planet. But the Space Race was still far from over.

President Kennedy wanted the United States to be the first nation to land people on the moon. At the time, the idea sounded like something out of science fiction. NASA worked

A replica of *Explorer I* hangs in the National Academy of Sciences in Washington, DC.

hard to achieve this goal and had its first successful moon landing in 1969. The United States became the first country to send people to the moon. Unfortunately, Kennedy did not live to see the moon landing. He was assassinated in 1963.

In the decades that followed, many other nations developed space programs. In 1998, the United

In addition to serving in the Navy and being a NASA astronaut, John Glenn was a senator for Ohio for 25 years.

Neil Armstrong and Buzz Aldrin, *pictured*, made history when they landed on the moon during the Apollo 11 mission.

States, Russia, and 13 other countries began working together to build the International Space Station (ISS). It took ten years and more than 30 missions to construct this laboratory that orbits Earth. Hundreds of people from around the world have spent time on the ISS.

As technology advanced, equipment on the ISS became outdated. Some parts of the structure have also worn out over time. By 2022, plans to build new space stations were in progress. NASA was also in the midst of the Artemis program, which aimed to return astronauts to the moon in the 2020s.

In December 2020, astronaut Mike Hopkins was sworn into the Space Force while aboard the ISS.

NASA AND THE SPACE FORCE

Both NASA and the Space Force are involved in space operations. However, they have some key differences. NASA is a civilian agency. The Space Force is a military branch that is organized under the Department of the Air Force.

NASA and the Space Force have different objectives. NASA is concerned with science and research. It uses satellites to learn more about Earth and space. It sends astronauts into orbit. The Space Force deals with the

A United Launch Alliance Atlas V rocket launched from Vandenberg Space Force Base in September 2021.

NASA launched a Telstar communications satellite in 1985. In 2022, about 63 percent of the satellites orbiting Earth were used for communication purposes.

military use of space. Its satellites are used for reconnaissance and communications. The Space Force also defends the computer networks related to these space systems.

Though NASA and the Space Force are separate agencies, the two sometimes work together. They share goals in establishing US space policy. The Space Force is working with

Many people work together to make sure that rocket launches are safe and successful.

NASA to ensure the safety of the Artemis missions and the astronauts involved.

The Space Force also partners with private space companies, such as SpaceX, to launch military satellites. Working with these companies helps the United States establish a strong presence in space. Private companies use Space Force bases to launch spacecraft related to national security.

THE WORK OF THE SPACE FORCE

Space technology has become a crucial part of modern life. Communications satellites carry radio and television signals to locations around the globe. Weather satellites gather data that helps improve weather forecasting and scientists' understanding of climate change. The satellites of the global positioning system (GPS) help with all kinds of navigation, providing location data for drivers of passenger cars, captains of massive ships, and practically everyone in between.

Software engineers write programs that guide spacecraft during launch and flight through space.

At the same time, space has never been more important to the military. The same GPS satellites that provide motorists with turn-by-turn directions help to accurately guide missiles and bombs. Communications satellites help military units talk to each other quickly and securely. Reconnaissance satellites

SpaceX launched a Falcon 9 rocket from a Space Force base in November 2021.

Satellites that orbit Earth help scientists track weather events.

give the military a clear overhead picture of enemy forces and structures. Warning satellites detect enemy missile launches as soon as they happen.

The job of the US Space Force is to protect all this vital equipment in Earth orbit, both for civilians and for the military. Members of the Space Force run rocket launch facilities on both the East and West coasts. They manage the operations of military satellites. They work to ensure that the United States continues to have free access to space.

ORGANIZATION OF THE SPACE FORCE

When the Space Force was formed in 2019, it became the first military branch to be added to the US armed forces since 1947. Although the branch is new, many of its members have a great deal of military experience. Air Force Space Command was

Space Force members perform routine checks to make sure satellites are operating properly.

Vice President Kamala Harris, *center*, greeted members of the US Space Force and US Space Command. Harris served as the chair of the National Space Council and was responsible for guiding US policy in space.

created in 1982 as a section of the Air Force. Members of Air Force Space Command were moved to the Space Force when that military branch was formed.

By 2023, more than 8,100 troops were part of the US Space Force, making it the smallest branch of the US military. About 75 percent of Space Force troops came from the Air Force. A small number of other military branch members have also transferred into the Space Force. About 7 percent of the Space

Force came from the Army. About 1 percent are former Navy members. And less than 1 percent came from the Marine Corps.

The Space Force also employs about 8,000 civilian workers. Although they are not military members, these individuals assist the Space Force. Some do this by performing work in science, aerospace, and engineering. Others do administrative work. The Space Force also has positions in intelligence, logistics, and leadership similar to those in other military branches.

Engineers working for the Space Force are expected to understand cutting-edge technology.

NOTABLE SPACE FORCE MEMBERS

General John W. "Jay" Raymond was sworn in as the first Chief of Space Operations for the Space Force in January 2020. Like many of the first members of this military branch, Raymond had previously served in the Air Force. He had been a commander in Air Force Space Command.

The Chief of Space Operations is responsible for overseeing the Space Force. The person in this position is expected to maintain the Space Force as an elite force that can protect US interests in space. He or she works to make sure the Space Force is equipped to quickly respond to threats.

General John W. Raymond gave a speech in August 2021 to officially establish the Space Systems Command unit within the Space Force.

Lieutenant General Nina Armagno smiles as family members pin her new rank insignia onto her uniform.

In August 2020, General Nina Armagno became a three-star general in the Space Force. Previously, Armagno had served as a lieutenant general in the Air Force. She was named the director of staff of the Space Force Headquarters at the Pentagon near Washington, DC. A ceremony was held to celebrate her move into this new role. During the ceremony, Raymond spoke of three qualities that made Armagno ideal for the job. He shared that she was a space expert, an experienced leader, and a generous mentor

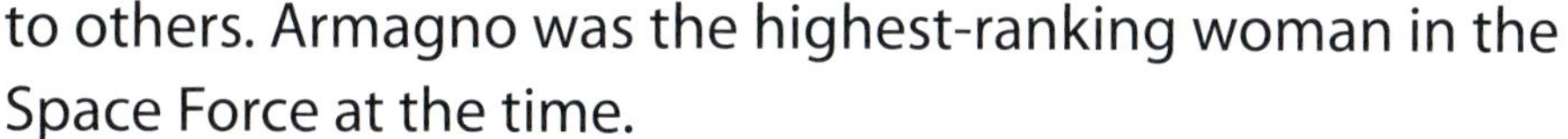

to others. Armagno was the highest-ranking woman in the Space Force at the time.

Lieutenant General B. Chance Saltzman, *center*, received the General Thomas D. White Space Award in 2021 when he was serving as Deputy Chief of Space Operations. This award recognizes a person's contributions to aerospace.

Raymond spent two and a half years leading the Space Force. He retired from service in November 2022. During a change-of-command ceremony that month, General B. Chance Saltzman became the new Chief of Space Operations. Like Raymond, he had moved to the Space Force after many years of service in the Air Force. He had also been the Deputy Chief of Space Operations under Raymond.

JOINING THE SPACE FORCE

In 2022, the Space Force received far more applications than there were available positions. For example, the Space Force announced that it was looking for cyber professionals. The branch received hundreds of applications. It hired only six people. Many qualified applicants had to be turned down.

People interested in applying to the Space Force should begin by taking the ASVAB. The minimum scores for jobs within this military branch vary. In general, recruits need a higher ASVAB score to serve in the Space Force than in other military branches.

Guardians must complete basic training that lasts for seven and a half weeks. This training includes instruction about space history and satellites.

Some 2020 graduates of the Air Force Academy joined the US Space Force.

Space Force Guardians may use virtual reality during their training.

Though many Guardians will work with technology, their boot camp still includes physical training. To graduate, Guardians must complete a 1.5-mile (2.4 km) run, push-ups, and sit-ups. They also learn to assemble and fire an M4 carbine.

Ranks within the Space Force begin with specialist 1 (E-1). Chief master sergeant (E-9) is the highest rank for

Security personnel practice running drills at Schriever Space Force Base in Colorado. This base monitors military satellite communications.

enlisted members. Officers start out as lieutenants or second lieutenants (O-1) and can rise to the rank of general (O-10).

Unlike other branches of the military, the Space Force does not have its own military academy. Graduates of the US Air

Force Academy can enter the Space Force as officers. People who have completed ROTC training also can become officers in the Space Force. The Space Force also has Officer Training School, where college graduates can study and learn skills that will allow them to be officers. This training lasts for nine and a half weeks.

Members of the Space Force who work in cyber operations should have strong computer skills.

GLOSSARY

aeronautical engineering
A field of engineering that deals with the design and operation of aircraft.

blockade
The act of using ships to prevent supplies from reaching enemy territory during a war or conflict.

civilian
A person who is not a member of the military.

classified
Secret and available only to certain high-ranking members of the military or government.

communism
A political system in which all property is owned by the government.

counterterrorism
Plans or safety measures that prevent or fight against terrorism.

covert
Not openly shown; secret.

decipher
To turn a secret or coded message back into readable form.

diplomacy
The practice of negotiating agreements between people or nations.

humanitarian
Relating to human welfare.

insurgent
Rebelling against an established government.

marksmanship
The ability to hit a target with a gun.

militia
An organized group of citizens that functions as a military force.

neutralize
To make ineffective or to eliminate a threat.

reconnaissance
An exploratory mission with the aim of gathering information, often in enemy territory.

TO LEARN MORE

FURTHER READINGS

Currie-McGhee, Leanne. *STEM Careers in the Military*. ReferencePoint, 2023.

Everything World War II: Facts and Photos from the Front Line to the Home Front! Collins, 2021.

Henzel, Cynthia Kennedy. *The War Encyclopedia*. Abdo, 2024.

ONLINE RESOURCES

To learn more about the US armed forces, please visit **abdobooklinks.com** or scan this QR code. These links are routinely monitored and updated to provide the most current information available.

INDEX

PHOTO CREDITS

Cover Photos: US Air Force, front (two planes, Air Force seal), back (three planes); Afro American Newspapers/Gado/Archive Photos/Getty Images, front (pilots); US Marine Corps, front (soldiers in boat, Marine Corps seal), back (soldiers); Nikolay Doychinov/AFP/Getty Images, front (tank and Army soldier); US Army, front (Army seal); US Coast Guard, front (Coast Guard seal); Ivan Cholakov/Shutterstock Images, front (helicopter and boat); US Navy, front (Navy seal); Glynnis Jones/Shutterstock Images, front (Navy sailors); US Space Force, front (Space Force seal, rocket launch); NASA, front (Mike Hopkins)

Interior Photos: US Air Force/DVIDS, 1, 6, 10–11, 12, 13, 18–19, 21, 24–25, 30, 31, 32, 33 (top), 33 (bottom), 34, 35, 36–37, 38, 39, 174, 175, 182; Spc. Michael Orton/DVIDS, 2–3, 71; Vernon Lewis Gallery/Stocktrek Images/Alamy, 4; US Air National Guard/DVIDS, 7, 18; US Air Force, 8, 9, 10, 14, 15, 16, 17, 86–87; Lawrence Crespo/DVIDS, 20; Everett Collection/Shutterstock Images, 22; Afro American Newspaper/Gado/Archive Photos/Getty Images, 23; US Department of Defense/AP Images, 24; Johannes Zoetekouw/Shutterstock Images, 26; Pictures from History/Universal Images Group/Getty Images, 27, 28, 153; Shutterstock Images, 29, 65, 76, 123; Photo 12/Universal Images Group/Getty Images, 40, 64; Popperfoto/Getty Images, 41; US Army/DVIDS, 42, 43, 48–49, 49, 50–51, 52–53, 68, 70; US Army, 44, 46, 47, 53, 54–55, 66; US Marine Corps, 45; Maj. Jeff Slinker/DVIDS, 51; Bettmann/Getty Images, 56 (top), 57, 61, 63, 67, 94; Pajor Pawel/Shutterstock Images, 56 (bottom); David Knox/Hulton Archive/Getty Images, 58; Stock Montage/Archive Photos/Getty Images, 59, 75; Chris Alcock/Shutterstock Images, 60; Harris & Ewing/Library of Congress, 62; Sgt. Amanda Hunt/DVIDS, 69; US Army Reserve/DVIDS, 72, 73; US Coast Guard/DVIDS, 74, 77, 78, 79, 80, 82, 83, 84, 84–85, 88, 91, 92, 96, 97, 99, 100, 101, 103, 104, 105, 106, 107; US Navy/DVIDS, 81, 112, 119, 135 (top), 137, 138–139, 140, 141, 143, 144, 145, 146, 147, 151, 152, 154, 155, 156, 160, 161, 162, 163, 165; US Coast Guard, 89, 98–99; US Navy, 90, 136, 142, 148, 149, 164; J. F. Jarvis/Archive Photos/Getty Images, 93; Universal History Archive/Universal Images Group/Getty Images, 95; Smith Collection/Gado/Archive Photos/Getty Images, 102, 157; US Marine Corps/DVIDS, 108, 109, 110–111, 111, 113, 114, 115, 116, 117, 118, 120, 121, 126, 128, 129, 130, 130–131, 132, 133; Mondadori Portfolio/Getty Images, 122; Sean Pavone/Shutterstock Images, 124; Corbis Historical/Getty Images, 125; Christian Petersen/Getty Images Sport/Getty Images, 127; MPI/Archive Photos/Getty Images, 134; Hulton Archive/Getty Images, 135 (bottom); Naval Special Warfare Command/DVIDS, 150; American Heroes Museum/Wikimedia Commons, 158; Peter Pereira/AP Images, 159; Al Drago/Bloomberg/Getty Images, 166; Samuel Corum/Pool/Getty Images News/Getty Images, 167; NASA, 168, 169, 170, 171, 172, 173, 177; US Space Force, 176; US Space Force/DVIDS, 178, 180, 181, 182–183, 184, 185, 186, 187; Mario Tama/Getty Images News/Getty Images, 179

ABDOBOOKS.COM
Published by Abdo Reference, a division of ABDO, PO Box 398166, Minneapolis, Minnesota 55439.

102023
012024

Editor: Angela Lim
Series Designer: Colleen McLaren
Production Designer: Karli Kruse

LIBRARY OF CONGRESS CONTROL NUMBER: 2023939660

PUBLISHER'S CATALOGING-IN-PUBLICATION DATA
Names: Gagne, Tammy, author.
Title: The armed forces encyclopedia / by Tammy Gagne
Description: Minneapolis, Minnesota: Abdo Reference, 2024 | Series: US military encyclopedias | Includes online resources and index.
Identifiers: ISBN 9781098293031 (lib. bdg.) | ISBN 9798384910978 (ebook)
Subjects: LCSH: Armed Forces--Juvenile literature. | Military, The--Juvenile literature. | Military history--Juvenile literature. | United States--Armed Forces--History--Juvenile literature. | Encyclopedias and dictionaries--Juvenile literature.
Classification: DDC 355.3--dc23